When Art isn't Real
The World's Most Controversial Objects under Investigation

When Art isn't Real

The World's Most Controversial Objects under Investigation

Andrew Shortland
Patrick Degryse

Leuven University Press

© 2022 by Leuven University Press / Presses Universitaires de Louvain / Universitaire Pers Leuven. Minderbroedersstraat 4, B-3000 Leuven (Belgium).

ISBN 978 94 6270 312 4
eISBN 978 94 6166 461 7 (epdf)
eISBN 978 94 6166 462 4 (epub)
https://doi.org/10.11116/9789461664617
D / 2022/ 1869 / 16
NUR: 682

Typesetting: Friedemann Vervoort
Cover design: Daniel Benneworth-Gray
Cover illustration: The Getty Kouros. Digital image courtesy of the Getty's Open Content Program.

Every effort has been made to contact all holders of the copyright to the visual material contained in this publication. Any copyright-holders who believe that illustrations have been reproduced without their knowledge are asked to contact the publisher.

.

Contents

Chapter 1
Introduction

In 2019, trade in the global art market was estimated to have been worth in excess of £50 billion. Around two thirds of that huge sum was traded in only two countries, the USA and the UK. China comes in third with an 18% share and, as with many China-related statistics, this share will only grow over the next few years. At the very top end of the market, the last decade has seen a huge rise in the prices paid for art. Of the top twenty most expensive paintings ever sold fifteen have been sold since 2010 and, remarkably, all ten of the top ten prices paid for paintings were paid in the last decade. This includes *Salvator Mundi*, attributed to Leonardo da Vinci, the world's most expensive painting and the subject of Chapter 7. It is interesting to note, therefore, that although the art market has such value, it is one of the least regulated markets in the world. The high values paid are often in cash, buyers and sellers largely relying on the "traditional … hand-shake culture of the art trade". This leads to the art market being called "famously opaque" with a threat of criminal activity that is ever present. The FBI has estimated that thieves steal art objects worth between $4-6 billion worldwide every year, raiding and damaging cultural assets. It identified art as the third biggest criminal market after drugs and weapons. Looted antiquities have been acknowledged by law enforcement bodies as a significant source of insurgent and terrorist funding.

The situation means a significant human institution, a basis of human culture and cultural identity made up of international networks of institutions such as museums, galleries, public exhibitions and auction houses, is blighted by crime. A survey of industry professionals conducted by Deloitte in 2016 reported that "around 75% of all stakeholders surveyed agree that 'authenticity, lack of provenance, forgery, and attribution' are the biggest threats to credibility and trust in the art market".

Despite this well-known prevalence of problems with forgeries, fakes and smuggled art objects, only limited resources have been committed by policing operations to dealing with art crime. This has led to greater pressure on business and cultural institutions to ensure that they are dealing in works with established provenance. It is this world that this book describes – the drive to protect a market from those who would want to profit from it illegally.

We both work in universities and are both career academics. We have approached the art world from the study of objects from the ancient world. We were both trained initially as geologists, but then fell under the spell of archaeology and the analysis of objects from Egypt and Rome. This is essentially curiosity-driven research, and we have the great luxury to be able to work with problems and objects as they tickle our fancy. Working on these materials and objects provides an opportunity to gather a database of workable scientific techniques and accurate chemical compositions, a body of knowledge on art and science that on the one hand can be used to comment on cultures of the past and human behaviour, but on the other can help to identify those objects that are more of the present than the past – fakes and forgeries. Working in university departments on historical objects, we both started initially by analysing excavated archaeological material. This was partly a matter of chance, but also reflected the way analysis was carried out twenty years ago. Then, to do any really accurate work, the necessity was to take samples from objects. This is much easier with excavated material which is usually already broken and/or fragmentary. However, the work quickly spread to analysing comparable collections in museums. It is in this way that we both were introduced for the first time to the buying and selling of objects on the art market. Museums, especially American museums, have always bought extensively from the market. There are a number of such examples in this book. They act as a caution as to what can go wrong when enthusiastic curators believe that they have discovered a "sleeper" – an important lost artefact, misidentified as something trivial in the past but actually of much greater historical (and, of course, financial) value. This book is a series of stories of objects where science has attempted to validate or repudiate the opinions of other experts. As we will see, some of the cases described here have been proved "beyond reasonable doubt", but others are still argued over, sometimes much to the chagrin of the scientists involved, for whom it is "case closed". In particular, with these stories we want to give the reader some feel for the people involved. A feel for those period or material experts who give their opinion on an object's validity from its looks, feel, even smell. A feel for the analysts, who employ their scientific equipment to the object and give their opinion from the numbers and pictures that are derived from them. A feel for the experts working with, in parallel with, and occasionally against each other.

Of course, it is also about the other side in this game, the forgers. We will show that some forgers have given a bit of insight into their motives. Surely, financial gain is one, perhaps very powerful reason to go about this work. However, it has been described by some as the motive to continue on the crooked path, not necessarily to start on it. Almost all *forgers* have more complex motives than just *financial* gain. Often there is an element of revenge in what they are doing. Sometimes they regard themselves as artistic geniuses who have cruelly and inexplicably been shunned by the art community. Therefore, there is an element of fooling and trying to embarrass those same critics and experts that have been dismissive of their own works. Once in the game, the forger can become addicted to the power he has. It becomes difficult to stop, and after all – when you're caught, you'll be famous and respected, or at least recognised, finally. There is also a great modern interest in newspapers and the public as a whole on the "little man" getting one over on the stuffy, élitist, upper classes of the art market – a forger can be a hero in the newspapers, despite what they are doing being essentially fraud.

Interestingly, most forgers claim to see many more of their works in museums and galleries, indistinguishable from the real thing, still unrecognised for the forgeries they really are – is this true, or are they just not able to get rid of that monkey on their shoulder, craving further attention, and recognition?

So there is a whole gamut of smoke and mirrors in this field – forgers routinely and, in some cases, pathologically lie. Some have lived so long with their untruths that they appear unable to distinguish fact from self-generated fiction. Not only that, but they are also responsive in their works – they tend to improve with time. Indeed, the arms race between those who forge and those who detect is rather exciting. It is also rather important – history is subtly changed by the insertion of fakes into an artist's or culture's oeuvre. Sometimes this is minor, sometimes (see Chapter 2, Piltdown Man) it can have major ramifications. However, always it is slowly changing, slowing subverting, history. Historians rightly strive for accuracy, even though all would accept that a lot is a matter of opinion. However, that opinion is more difficult if some of the evidence used to create it is unreliable, corrupted by forgers' intent on personal gain or fame, the effect of which is that they are, bit by bit, poisoning history.

Throughout the book we describe scientific approaches and briefly some methods, our area of expertise after all. However, individual chapters deal with personal stories related to the objects, and how they make or break careers and people. In the end, this book is also about how we interact with the objects and the people. Each chapter discusses a particular case, usually with one object or related group of objects taking centre stage. Often, we try to contrast this object with other similar cases. We also draw out themes present in most if not all of the cases we discuss, each theme brought out more strongly in one of the particular stories.

Our first case study in chapter 2 carries the title Piltdown Man and deals with our earliest case and one of the most famous. Piltdown is the location where a hominid skull was found, and it must be one of the oldest objects ever to be deliberately faked, dating as it does to before modern *Homo sapiens* walked the earth. In this story a very senior, world renowned scientist appears to have been fooled by an extremely prolific amateur forger. The themes that come out of this chapter are twofold. Firstly, the forgery here had a massive and long-term impact on our interpretation of the ancient past. It threw history off track for decades and caused our interpretation of real hominid remains to be distorted and reassessed. However, this is also the story of a senior scientist whose name will forever be tarnished by association with the case. Whatever wonderful work he did in other areas, it is with this case that his name is most known. He never lived to know that his prize discovery was an outrageous, deliberate lie perpetrated by a man whom he regarded as a friend.

Chapter 3, the Getty Kouros, also discusses an ancient object, in this case a Greek stone statue. Here the story is, if anything, more complex than in Chapter 2. The case becomes not only a question whether the object is a modern forgery, but also a discussion of how such an object, if real, could end up in an American museum. It shows that in some cases the work of the forger and the work of the looter and trafficker are closely related, each using the other as cover for their activities. The chapter discusses the murky world of trafficking in looted antiquities and how, in the past, some august institutions adopted a light-handed attitude towards the investigation of the history of objects that they wished to acquire.

After the controversy about the potential for recently smuggled or forged objects that is the heart of Chapter 3, the next chapter deals with the Turin Shroud, an object which all concerned agree has existed in pretty much its current state since at least the fourteenth century AD. If forged, it is therefore the earliest forgery in this volume. These are perhaps only facts that all agree on in this, perhaps most argued over of all the cases we present. For this is a religious object, intimately connected (or not) with the person of Jesus Christ. In chapter 4 we discuss how difficult it can be to approach objects, especially religious objects, objectively. How difficult it is for some to accept that scientists working on such objects are driven not by a desire to corrupt or deceive believers, but simply by an interest in the right answer. Of all the cases covered, this provokes the strongest opinions (on both sides) and the most vituperative arguments. There will almost certainly never be a consensus on this, one of the most emotive, interesting and charismatic objects ever made, regardless of whether it is real or a medieval forgery.

In contrast, chapter 5 on the Vinland Map presents an object that has much more of an academic discussion behind it. Potentially an early map mentioning North America, this has far less of the emotional impact of the previous chapter. However, the theme developed here is the ability of scientists to argue amongst themselves over the same observation or series of data. It shows how a clever forgery (if that is what it is), even if relatively simply made, can have generations of scientists scratching their heads and changing their minds. And, once again, there is a significant impact on our understanding of history if the object is real.

The modern case of the "Amarna Princess", a small stone statue presumed of ancient Egyptian origin, is presented in chapter 6. It is the first case where the forger is still very much alive. So alive in fact that he has published his memoirs, showing a wide range of different object types that he forged. Here the theme is that of the forger's mindset and motivation. It concerns an individual who extorted millions from victims and yet does not seem at all interested in the money. That individual also was relatively untrained – not a graduate of an art school or famous university (indeed, of any university – he left school at 16) – and yet with great artistic skill and even more operational cunning. He and his family worked a complex series of forgeries and deceptions for over a decade; indeed the extent of his forgeries is still debated and he has made incredible claims to having forged some very important and expensive pieces, also connecting him to the next chapter.

Chapter 7, Leonardo and the Eye, talks about the work of Leonardo da Vinci in general, and one or two of his paintings in particular. How much contact does an artist like Leonardo have to have with a painting for it to be a "Leonardo"? A lot of artists worked in studios with their students – is it enough for Leonardo to paint just part of the image? This is also a story of the huge amounts of money that can be made on the art market by the right person at the right time. It is the story of how the opinion of one or two individuals, combined with some very astute marketing, can make $100 million in only a few years. This is broadened into the theme of connoisseurs – who are these strange people who can just look at an object and know that it is real? What is "the eye", that mystical ability to just know that an object is right? It also explores what happens when this whole edifice comes crashing down and a famous connoisseur makes a howling and very public mistake.

Chapter 8 the Reconstruction of Knossos continues on from the previous chapter in its investigation of how much of an object has to be created by an artist for it to be his or hers. Here the emphasis changes to how much of an object has to be preserved to make the object still the object it was? The art of conservation and restoration is described and different ideas of the ethically permissible extent of reconstruction is considered. Finally, this is taken to an extreme when an archaeological site is discussed where a very high percentage of the visible remains are extensively, and sometimes imaginatively, reconstructed. How much of this can go on before the site has all the historically damaging effects of a forgery?

The final chapters bring us to a conclusion, but also provide a useful bibliography and glossary. Rather than providing exhaustive references through the chapters, we hope that the guided bibliography is a more user friendly way of exploring further the cases and themes raised in this book. The bibliography details some of the best sources that we have used in the drawing together of the chapters. A short commentary is provided on each of the sources, the aim here being to help readers pick a reference that is useful for them, whether they want a technical report or more general work, an "accepted" version of events or a more controversial one. In this way, readers will know whether the text they are reading is widely praised or "fake news". Finally, a short glossary is added for the specialist terms, techniques and individuals named in the text, once again to free the main text of explanations that might interfere with the narrative.

The research, writing and travel for this book have taken the two of us over a decade and we have worked on many of the areas in collaboration. However, some of the experiences, impressions and descriptions are more personal to each of us – this is especially true of meetings where we have not both been present. We have tried to give a flavour of this through asides which we have written as individuals. To delineate this, they are set in a different font.

The authors would like to acknowledge the help that they have received from the following academic colleagues and others in the research for this book: Heather Bonney, Mark Carnall, Ian Trumble, Pierrette Squires, Stephen Donovan, Ray Swan and Sophie Hayes. Several others would prefer to remain nameless, but are thanked here. A special note should be made of Katherine Eremin and Marc Walton for many years of travel, hospitality and debate. Parts of this book were devised and written during PdG's visiting fellowship at All Souls College, Oxford.

Chapter 2
Piltdown Man

A job vacancy at the British Museum.

On 25 March 1882, the above job advertisement for a museum assistant appeared in the magazine *The Field*. To modern eyes this is an odd place to put such an advertisement, for *The Field* still exists and is the archetypal "hunting, shooting, fishing" magazine. It is also the oldest such magazine, having been in continual publication since 1853. However, *The Field* has interested its readers with wider matters, ranging from reports from the Crimean War to the development of the rules of lawn tennis. Perhaps, in this context, the advertisement is not so odd. It tells of two vacant situations as assistants at the British Museum, one "First Class" in the Department of

Minerals, one "Second Class" in the Department of Geology, with annual starting salaries of £250 and £120 respectively. At a time when a skilled carpenter or bricklayer might earn £100 pounds per year and the most junior army officer £200, these are adequate, but not generous, amounts (rumour has it that some museums still do not pay top salaries…). However, the advertisement makes it clear that there is the opportunity for this to grow annually.

The British Museum mentioned here is the then brand new "British Museum (Natural History)", abbreviated as BM(NH). The British Museum itself was founded as a "universal museum" by the British Museum Act 1753, joining together several libraries and collections of curiosities including fossils, rocks, antiquities, dried plants, animals and birds, ethnographic materials, books, manuscripts, drawings and much besides. The beautiful neo-classical buildings and courtyard in Bloomsbury in North London that the museum still occupies were finished in the 1850s. However, there was nowhere near enough space for all the collections, so the natural history collections were to be moved out and into a new building in Kensington in the up-and-coming West of London. Although completed only 30 years or so after the British Museum proper, the BM(NH) was a completely different building, reflecting the very latest tastes of late Victorian England. It was designed as a huge, Neo-Gothic, almost "cathedral", in coloured brick and stone, a design that split opinion then as it does now. It opened in 1881, so had been open only months when our advertisement appeared in press. A major role of the desired new staff would be to move the natural history collections from the old museum in Bloomsbury to Kensington and to design the displays – the BM(NH) had opened with a lot of empty space in its display rooms.

These two posts, although junior, would be prestigious, with access to the world's greatest collections, top scientists and the opportunity to progress. In the Victorian world it is very likely that such posts would be filled by the protégés of the Head of the Museum, or by young men with political influence. Indeed, the successful candidate would need to have a letter of recommendation from one of only three Principal Trustees of the British Museum: the Archbishop of Canterbury, the Lord Chancellor or the Speaker of the House of Commons! Additionally, the Head of the Geology Department, in museums known as the "Keeper", certainly had in mind a person who had worked with him for years – a strong favourite. However, the Keeper was told that the posts must be filled by examination, so there was just a chance for outsiders.

Arthur Woodward was shown the advertisement by his father. He was two months short of his eighteenth birthday, so actually underage for the jobs. Arthur had wanted to join the Geological Survey in Australia, but this had just been vetoed by his parents. Transportation of convicts to Australia finished only in 1868, so perhaps his father and mother still associated this new country with that. Perhaps it was in a spirit of reconciliation that they showed Arthur this, more suitable, post. Arthur had several disadvantages in applying for this role. He was from Macclesfield, a textile town in Northern England (you can almost hear the Keeper saying "Where?"), not the fashionable South-East or, better still, London. His parents could not give him an easy introduction into the world of science and he had not been to the University of Oxford or Cambridge. He did not have a great deal of influence, having to go through a tortuous series of local dignitaries before eventually getting the Archbishop to support his application. However, he did have a couple of big advantages. The Keeper was told that the posts must be filled by examination, to avoid the appearance of appointing favoured, placed men. Arthur was talented and committed, and the examination saw him come top (beating the Keeper's man, eight years his senior, into fourth place). The job, assistantship second class in the Department of Geology, was his.

It did not start well. The Keeper perhaps nursed some resentment and made it clear that Arthur was on a year's probation. And there was another complication. The Keeper's name was Henry Woodward (absolutely no relation, as I am sure he grew tired of telling people), and to avoid "confusion" insisted that Arthur changed his surname, so Arthur became Arthur Smith Woodward, incorporating his mother's maiden name. There is an image of the BM(NH) Geology Department staff taken in 1883, a year after Smith Woodward joined. Smith Woodward is the tall young man standing on the left, sporting a neat beard, which he wore for his entire life, and a rather dashing double-breasted suit. The suit is perhaps new – it fits well and is neat and clean, in contrast to the dusty and threadbare look sported by his seniors in the picture. The Keeper, Henry Woodward, sits on the right, a serious-looking man with an unsympathetic eye. The other three members of staff could be straight out of central casting for Victorian *paterfamilias*. They are all pictured in one of the cloistered courtyards of the new Museum, with the multicoloured brick clearly visible.

Staff of the new British Museum (Natural History) in a court within the building. Arthur Smith Woodward is standing on the left. His boss, Henry Woodward, is seated on the right.

© The Trustees of the Natural History Museum, London.

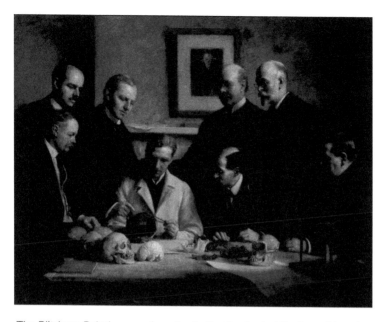

The Piltdown Painting, now hanging in the Geological Society of London in Burlington House, Piccadilly. Smith Woodward stands on the far right. Standing next to him is Dawson. Keith sits in the white laboratory coat.
Reproduced by permission of the Geological Society of London.

Let us now fast forward over thirty years to another image, this time an oil painting, finished in 1915 and now hanging in the Geological Society of London in Burlington House on Piccadilly. This is the famous Piltdown Painting and, again, it is a collection of learned men, eight this time, some seated, some standing. Arthur Smith Woodward is pictured standing on the right. He was fifty at the time the picture was painted, but looks older, his hair and beard grey to white, and he is balding (he lost his hair in his early twenties). He wears a pair of pince-nez glasses with a gold chain and he looks quite old-fashioned compared to many of the others, who wear modern-looking suits. In this image, the eyes of all the men, and also those of the viewer, are drawn to the table that they cluster around. A single figure in the middle wears a white laboratory coat and holds what looks like a slightly deflated brown leather football in his right hand and a pair of dividers in the left. Just in case the viewer is in any doubt that this is the important part of the painting, one of the standing men is pointing at it – rather heavy-handed imagery by the artist, John Cooke. The table has a number of skulls on it and a wooden contraption designed to allow skulls to be measured. The skull on the right, on its own, is that of an ape. The four skulls on the left are modern human. The brown "football" is pictured between the two, but closer to the modern human; again some rather heavy-handed imagery, for the "football" is also a skull, a reconstructed cast of the brown fragments of cranium and jaw that also lie on the table. The skull fragments and cast are shown between the ape and human skulls because the men pictured believed this to be the most important find in British palaeoanthropology – the "missing link" in the evolution from ape to man. Its importance is highlighted by the ghostly image shown in the frame above the fireplace in the background – Charles Darwin, father of evolutionary theory hovers ethereally above the scene.

This is the famous Piltdown skull, and the men shown in the picture all contributed to its finding, study and conservation. All would gain from their association with the skull; no fewer than four of them would be knighted for their services to science. However all is not as it might seem, for it is extremely likely that at least one of the men pictured here knows that this skull is not the missing link. He knows this because he himself made the skull, fraudulently and deliberately, with the intent of deceiving the other men around the table and the world in general. For Piltdown is a fake – an outrageous concoction that fooled British academia for the best part of forty years. It would damage Smith Woodward's career and tarnish his exceptional legacy. It would set British palaeoanthropology back so far that it almost didn't recover.

The first finds

For Arthur Smith Woodward, his involvement with Piltdown started on 15 February 1912. By now he had a very successful career, had published widely and well in his specialist area of fossil fish, and had risen to be Head of Geology – he was now the Keeper – at the BM(NH). On this particular morning he received a letter from an acquaintance, Charles Dawson, who was a solicitor and amateur fossil collector. Dawson stands next to Smith Woodward in the painting. He is also balding and wears glasses. He has almost a fatherly appearance, apparently pleased that the learned men around the table are paying the skull such attention. Dawson and Smith Woodward had been out collecting together in a quarry near Hastings and the letter discussed the expenses that they had incurred. It also mentioned Arthur Conan Doyle (the author of the Sherlock Holmes stories) who was writing a new novel, *Lost World*, but was also a fossil enthusiast known to both men. There was more chat about mutual friends and colleagues and their activities until Dawson casually mentioned a find that one might imagine immediately caught Smith Woodward's attention. He said:

> "I have come across a very old Pleistocene (?) bed [...] which I think is going to be interesting. It has a lot of iron-stained flints in it, so I suppose it is the oldest known flint gravel in the Weald. I portion [*sic*] of human skull which will rival H. Heidelbergensis in solidity".

A "Pleistocene bed" refers to a layer of rock or, as in this case, gravel of Pleistocene age which, using modern scientific dating, we know to be somewhere between 11,000 and 2.6 million years old. Dawson and Smith Woodward would have had only the haziest idea of the calendrical date. The Weald is an area of chalk uplands in Southern England stretching across the counties of Hampshire, Surrey, Sussex and Kent. The key sentence is the last one. It is slightly garbled, but suggests that Dawson has found an ancient, thick fragment of hominid skull similar to that of *Homo Heidelbergensis* – "Heidelberg man". Found near the German city of Heidelberg, this was an ape-like jaw with teeth and represented the most likely earliest ancestor of modern humans, *Homo sapiens,* then known. Dawson had had the chance to see casts of this fossil specimen, although it is not known when, and so he knew what he was talking about in the comparison. At the time, France and Germany had a wealth of early hominid fossils, including Neanderthal man, *Homo neanderthalensis.* Britain, on the other hand, had a rather paltry selection of questionable stone tools, known as eoliths and palaeoliths (now dismissed as entirely natural), but precious little else. French palaeontologists jokingly referred to their British colleagues as "chasseurs de cailloux", or "pebble hunters", and that smarted with the British. Britain needed some good fossils to keep up with continental Europe. Could this be what Dawson had found?

Smith Woodward wrote back to Dawson by return of post, apparently suggesting that he keep quiet about the find until Smith Woodward had had chance to see it. Weather and work commitments intervened, which meant that Smith Woodward could not go down to Sussex to see the site or the fossil as he obviously wanted to do. Dawson, perhaps overcome in the excitement of his find, starts to show it to a range of friends and colleagues and this is recorded in contemporary letters during April. Eventually on 24 May Dawson comes to London and, perhaps with a degree of theatre, places the skull on Smith Woodward's desk. Smith Woodward must have been delighted, for it would be obvious to him that the skull was indeed a hominid. We can be sure that he asked Dawson the exact circumstances of its discovery, the details of which Dawson repeats in one of his later papers in the *Hastings and Sussex Naturalist.* It appears that Dawson was a visitor to a Barkham Manor, an estate near the hamlet of Piltdown and a couple of miles west of the Sussex town of Uckfield. Dawson was working in the Manor as president of the Court Baron, a junior version of a magistrates' court designed to hear disputes of tenants and the like. Whilst on site, he visited some pits where gravel was extracted to put onto the farm tracks. The farm hands digging the gravel told him that they had never found any "fossils or bones", but Dawson asked them to look out for anything that might be of interest. Dawson does not say exactly when this conversation occurred, but it is likely to have been in 1899. On a subsequent visit (perhaps in 1908), workman handed him the first piece of skull, part of the left parietal. He immediately searched for more, but could not find anything. "Several years later" (in 1911) he found a "larger piece of the same skull". In his book *The Earliest Englishman*, Smith Woodward gives a slightly different version of the find, which he could only have had from Dawson himself. He says that the workmen "dug up what they thought was a coconut", which they thought might interest Dawson. However, since it was "a little bulky to keep, they broke it and threw away all but one piece". The story is repeated in other accounts, all of which derive directly or indirectly from Dawson.

There are some obvious problems with these accounts of the first finding of the skull. The "coconut" story does not feature in Dawson's formal accounts – perhaps this was the verbal story behind the formal account. More difficult is the timeframe – it takes the labourers eight years to find something and, in the coconut story, the first thing they do is smash it with a shovel and throw away most of it. Why did Dawson never mention the early first find of the skull in 1908 to Smith Woodward (or anyone else) even though they were fossil hunting together in the same area? The second fragment is not found for another three to four years, and yet is this the same skull? Why does Smith Woodward appear not to question the various discrepancies in Dawson's account?

Down to Piltdown, the 1912 season

As Smith Woodward looked at the fragments of fossil skull on his desk on 24 May 1912, he knew that this was perhaps the find of his career. Both he and Dawson were impatient to get down to the site and look for more, but had to wait for the pits to dry out after recent rain. Therefore it was on 2 June that they eventually made it to the site. They were accompanied by Father Marie-Joseph Pierre Teilhard de Chardin, a Jesuit priest and keen amateur palaeontologist, who had worked before with Dawson looking for fossils in the area, plus an unknown man who "was there to help us dig". This was probably Venus Hargreaves, a labourer who was employed by the team in 1912 and 1913 and appears in some of the photographs of the diggings. They dug and sorted the gravels sporadically at weekends and holidays through June, July and August, but unfortunately either kept no notebooks of the dig, or the notebooks were lost or destroyed subsequently. What was found, and when, therefore has to be reconstructed from contemporary letters or later accounts, often muddled. What is clear is that they were exceptionally lucky to have a spectacular success on the first day, even though they apparently did not arrive on site until 3pm. A letter from Teihard de Chardin, written *the next day* clearly states that after "several hours [...] Dawson discovered a new fragment of the famous human skull". A few weeks later, three more conjoining fragments of the same skull were found on successive days. According to Smith Woodward they were "evidently not [...] disturbed since they were thrown away", echoing his coconut story.

The real prize also came sometime in June, but again it is not clear when. For the first time in undisturbed gravel (rather than in the spoil from digging), Dawson found a further fossil fragment. However, this time it was a piece of the jaw, which allowed it to be directly compared to *H. heidelbergensis* for the first time. Dawson said that it was found in the identical spot to the very first find, years before. Smith Woodward then found another piece of cranium "within a yard" of where the jaw was found. In addition to the hominid bones, a diverse collection of animal bones including mastodon, hippopotamus, deer, horse and elephant were found, along with now discredited "worked" flints, all naturally stained brown by the iron content of the gravel.

This completed the first season at Piltdown, and Dawson and Smith Woodward sat down to study what they had found and to draft a formal announcement of the discovery. At this point the first and only attempt at chemical analysis was carried out. Dawson sent a small fragment of bone from the cranium to Samuel Allinson Woodhead, who was "Public Analyst for East Sussex and Hove, and Agricultural Analyst for East Sussex". Dawson had worked with him several times before and Woodhead was familiar with the Piltdown site. His chemical analysis showed that the bone contained no organic material, but high contents of phosphates and iron. The fragment was therefore fossilised, not fresh bone – good news. The jaw was not analysed. The paper was ready for publication.

> *We also wanted to go down to Piltdown, and by a remarkable coincidence came across a guide to the sites of the area written by Prof. Stephen Donovan, who works in the Naturalis Museum, a few buildings down the road from where I teach at Leiden University, a gentleman and a geologist. A brief exchange of messages quickly led to a coffee and an amicable chat about our mutual interest in Piltdown Man and the people involved. He was clear about which of the eight men in the picture was guilty, but amazed how geological evidence at least putting big question marks besides the 'fossils' was simply ignored.*
>
> *At the time of the Piltdown Man discovery, Steve described Barkham Manor, where the fossils were found, was "a magnet for the curious". Though within reach of London, it was always a slightly inaccessible site. Yet on 12 July 1913 a field trip of close to a hundred attendees was organised to the site by the Geologists' Association, led by the experts, Charles Dawson and Arthur Smith Woodward – a field day for them both!*
>
> *As we were particularly interested in the type locality of Piltdown Man, marked by a memorial stone but on private property, Steve provided us with the contact details of the owners of the land. Advance arrangements had to be made, but it quick-*

ly became clear that access to the memorial stone was not going to be easy. When emails remained unanswered, the classic phone call was tried. We were politely kept at bay. It seems today that a lot of people still want to see the site, and managing such visits is not popular. So the memorial stone remained protected by iron gates and a 'Private No Trespassers' sign. We were to be allowed only a distant glimpse... as the gates opened to let in the proprietors/guests in a 1930s Bentley. Perhaps some people are fed up with the Piltdown story? Another site we wanted to see was The Piltdown Man pub, which lies on the main A272 road, just a short walk over the fields from Barkham Manor. We arrived for lunch to find an establishment completely deserted, apart from the bar tender. The pub had changed its name to the rather unexciting "The Lamb", with the bar tender having only the haziest idea that the pub had a previous name, and what it meant. There was no reference to the famous skull that we could see. Again, it seemed that the story was not popular locally, and incidentally we've learnt that the empty "Lamb" then also closed. However, just as this book is published, we learn that it has reopened with the name "Piltdown Man" again, hopefully this will bring the new owners, Fraser and Annie luck.

The find announced

Somehow the story of the finds leaked out before publication. An anonymous source gave details of the find to the *Manchester Guardian*, which on 21 November ran the headline "The Earliest Man? Remarkable Discovery in Sussex". The newspaper knew that the find was from a gravel pit and speculated immediately that this could be "the missing link" in the evolution "from the highest apes and the lowest men". It is easy to imagine Dawson and Smith Woodward's irritation that their work could be announced before they were ready for it, scooping them. Journalists descended on the BM(NH) and Smith Woodward was forced to confirm that the story was correct and that the formal announcement would be made soon. In the end, it was made on 18 December 1912 to the Geological Society in Burlington House, where the painting still hangs. The meeting room was packed to the rafters, and the presentation was given in three parts. First, Dawson gave the background to the discovery, the geology of the gravels in which the finds were found and the details of the first season's work. This was followed by Smith Woodward's account of the reconstruction of the skull, which was shown in public for the first time. Smith Woodward was in no doubt that the cranium was "essentially human", but the "mandible appears to be almost precisely that of an ape". He proposed that this represented a new genus for the hominid line, which he christened *Eoanthropus dawsoni*, "Dawson's dawn man" in honour of its finder.

Third to speak was Grafton Elliot Smith, Professor of Anatomy at Manchester University. Elliot Smith is also depicted in the painting – he is the younger man who is pointing to the skull, perhaps indicating some feature that the others had missed. This is appropriate, because Elliot Smith was one of the few present who had had a chance to study the fossil before the meeting. He had taken a cast of the braincase of the skull (pictured in white and placed centrally on the table in the painting) and his talk was on the shape of the brain of *Eoanthropus*. His study of the brain led him to believe that *Eoanthropus* was able to speak and "had the ability to recall names".

The presentation was in general well received, everyone understanding the importance of the finds. However, there was a good deal of discussion on two points: the age of the fossil and the accuracy of its reconstruction. The presentation had specified that the gravels (and therefore the skull) were Pleistocene. However, while some in the audience thought that they could be as early as Pliocene (up to 5 million years old on modern dating), others thought they could be considerably younger. Given that the understanding of the absolute ages of these deposits was poor at the time, this was largely speculation. In terms of the events that followed, the questions about the reconstruction are more important. The first comments were made by Edwin Ray Lankester, by then retired, but previously

Professor of Zoology at University College London, then Professor of Anatomy at Oxford and finally Keeper of Zoology at the BM(NH). He was therefore an ex-colleague of Smith Woodward's, having run another of the Museum's departments for eight years. It is perhaps natural therefore that Smith Woodward had given Lankester the opportunity to examine the fossil a few weeks before the presentation. Lankester is the large man with the full head of hair who is seated at the extreme right of the Piltdown Painting. He broadly agreed with the reconstruction that Smith Woodward had produced, although later admitted to some doubt as to whether the jaw and the cranium belonged together. He had some comments on the shape of the jaw and how it related to the rest of the skull, but was broadly happy. From such an influential and well-placed man, this support was important.

A further highly placed academic and major player made another significant comment on the presentation. This was Arthur Keith, who was Conservator at the Hunterian Museum of the Royal College of Surgeons and an important academic anatomist. He also questioned the reconstruction, especially of the jaw, which he thought "approached too nearly the characters of the chimpanzee". He thought the shape of the jaw and the way it connected to the skull would preclude the animal being able to speak. Not only that, but the ape-like nature of the jaw made it, in Keith's opinion, likely to be very old, supporting those who from studying the gravels placed them in the Pliocene. However, if *Eoanthropus* was the maker of the supposed primitive tools that they had found associated with it, then in Keith's view the jaw could not be as apelike as the reconstruction suggested. Arthur Keith is the central figure in the Piltdown Painting, holding the reconstruction and wearing the white lab coat. The final important comment was made by David Waterston, an anatomist from King's College London. He had severe doubts that the jaw and the cranium belonged to the same animal. He could not see how the jaw would articulate, as the skull was so much like that of a man, but the jaw too close to that of a chimpanzee. Other comments talked again about the dating, with a whole range of possibilities suggested from an interpretation of the gravels. Despite some misgivings, the consensus of the meeting, reported in newspapers of the time, was that the Dawson and Smith Woodward presentation and reconstruction were compelling, and few doubted that this was the most important hominid fossil find ever made in Britain and at least of equal importance to those from the continent. England had its important fossil at last.

The Piltdown fossils are still in the BM(NH), under the care of the Dr Heather Bonney, the Principal Curator of Human Remains and Anthropology. The BM(NH) has only a tiny fraction of its objects on display and only a small part of the Museum is open to the public. Beyond locked doors throughout the public Museum there is a whole second, larger Museum full of stores, stacks, offices, laboratories and above all drawer upon countless drawer of museum specimens. Heather was very kind in meeting us and taking us through one of these "Alice in Wonderland" doors to the curators' world beyond. Her office was a treasure trove of objects under study and ongoing projects, and amongst them, for our benefit, were the Piltdown fragments. I have been very familiar with copies and casts of the pieces, indeed I have some that sit permanently on my desk, so it was interesting to see how the "real" pieces compared. Obviously, my mindset was completely the opposite of that of the poor gentlemen in the Piltdown painting – I knew certainly that this was a fake, whereas most of them had no reason at all to suspect that it was. However, the fragments did seem very artificial, they did not feel "right". Perhaps they have deteriorated in the hundred years since they were found, but the tooth especially really looks painted. It is amazing, as we will discuss often in this book, how wanting or needing to believe unconsciously changes the way you see the World. How else was one of the world's most pre-eminent palaeontologists fooled?

New reconstruction and the 1913 season

In April 1913, Dawson and Smith Woodward's paper announcing the discovery of Piltdown was formally published in the *Quarterly Journal of the Geological Society of London*. This date corresponded with the first casts of the skull to be available commercially. You could buy a set from Damon Company of Weymouth for the princely sum of nine pounds and seventeen shillings – for an extra two pounds and ten shillings you could have copies of some of the "stone tools" as well. Arthur Keith, one of the critics at the meeting in Burlington House, was one of the first to buy a set. He was convinced that the reconstruction was wrong, and that such a modern-looking skull could not be reconstructed in such an apelike way. Smith Woodward's reconstruction showed a complete skull that probably meant that the *Eoanthropus* did not walk upright. Keith could not believe that this was the case, given the size and shape of the cranium. He thought the cranium was better reconstructed with a much larger capacity, up to 1500 cubic centimetres, much more that Smith Woodward's 1070 cm^3, and well within the range of a modern human. There were two fundamental problems when it came to trying to fit the cranium and the jaw together. The first was that the condylar process, the part of the mandible that articulated with the rest of the skull, was broken off, giving no clear idea how this might have worked. Secondly, the front of the jaw was missing too. This meant that it was unclear whether the jaw was pronounced, like that of an ape, or relatively flat fronted, like that of a modern human. A key indicator of this could have been the mandible incisor tooth, but this was missing. If it were large and projecting, then the ape reconstruction was correct, but if smaller, then the flat-fronted, manlike reconstruction would be better. Unfortunately, as G.S. Miller pointed out a little later in 1915, "deliberate malice could hardly have been more successful than the hazards of deposition in so breaking the fossils as to give free scope to individual judgement in fitting the parts together". More fossil fragments were needed.

Keith pursued his more manlike reconstruction and eventually showed it in an exhibition at the Royal College of Surgeons, where he worked. The reconstruction looks remarkably manlike and Keith proposed a different name for the fossil – *Homo piltdownensis,* or "man of Piltdown". He could not agree with Smith Woodward and Dawson that this fossil needed a completely new genus, *Eoanthropus* – to Keith this was a man, this was *Homo.* What Dawson thought of his surname disappearing from the fossil name is unfortunately not recorded, although he does seem to have sent the *Daily Express* a slightly joking riposte, which was published on 15 August 1913. He uses the pseudonym "Eoanthropus dawsoni" and humorously suggests that he would have "not the slightest objection to being called *Homo Keithii*" – "Keith's man"! Nevertheless, the potential loss of his name from the fossil must have stung.

Fortunately, as this debate was going on, Dawson and Smith Woodward were again digging intermittently on the site, as their time allowed. They uncovered more broken flints, but no further hominid parts. On 9 August they were joined by Father Teilhard de Chardin and by Smith Woodward's wife, Maude, and this brought them more luck. Dawson found, again in the gravel disturbed by the workmen, two fragments of hominid nasal bones. These fitted with either of the reconstructions, so did not add much to the story. What was really needed was that canine tooth. What happened next is therefore truly remarkable. On 30 August, only two weeks after Dawson's jokey letter to the *Daily Express*, they were working again on the site. Either Dawson or Smith Woodward (or both, it is un-clear) suggested to Teilhard de Chardin that he take a short break and look through some of the recently dug gravel which had been washed by the rain. There, on the surface, he "very soon" found the missing canine tooth. This was an incredibly lucky find, and it was immediately obvious to them all that the tooth was large and therefore favoured Smith Woodward's reconstruction of an ape-like *Eoanthropus*, not Keith's *Homo.* This was a fitting climax to the 1913 season, and Smith Woodward again planned to keep it quiet and announce it after proper study. Unfortunately, however, the story was again leaked, this time to the *Daily Express*, the very paper to which Dawson had sent his letter. The story was published on 2 September, and Dawson wrote to Smith Woodward saying that he was "very annoyed about it". Once again Smith Woodward had journalists contacting him, but it did mean that there was a good crowd for the formal announcement, made to the British Association in Birmingham. Smith Woodward now had more evidence for his version of the reconstruction – for *Eoanthropus dawsoni*, and the argument swung in his favour. Dawson kept his name on the fossil.

"Barcombe Mills Man"

However, we cannot leave 1913 behind without mentioning one oddity. In July, Dawson wrote again to Smith Woodward saying that he had found the remains of a second prehistoric hominid, not at Piltdown, but in the gravels near the River Ouse near Barcombe Mills, five miles to the south. According to Dawson, the skull fragment he had was not as thick as *E. Dawsoni*, "but it may be a descendant". Smith Woodward saw the fragment in Uckfield the next day, but what he thought of it was never recorded. Indeed, neither Dawson nor Smith Woodward ever published the paper on the skull, or even mentioned it in one of the high-profile presentations. We will return to Barcombe Mills Man later.

1914 – doubts and bats

The reconstruction argument continued through to 1914, with Keith and Grafton Elliot Smith acting as champions for the *Homo* and *Eoanthropus* interpretation respectively. It became heated; the argument was a "disgusting mess" according to Elliot Smith, and the cause of the end of their friendship, according to Keith. However, there were also very significant rumblings from across the Atlantic. William King Gregory, a palaeontologist at the American Museum of Natural History, wrote an article that included a mention of *Eoanthropus*. In it he suggested that it had been "suggested by some" that the *Eoanthropus* fossil was "not old at all; that they may even represent a deliberate hoax [...] 'planted' in the gravel bed to fool the scientists". This is the first mention of Piltdown Man being a hoax, but we have no clue who the "some" who had suggested this might be.

> *I have a particular fondness for the story of the Piltdown cricket bat. Sometimes in the investigation of fakes and forgeries the story becomes so surprising it is difficult to believe that the story itself is not completely fabricated, let alone the fragments that are being discussed. Sometimes, if you wrote it in a fictional novel, people would put the book down saying that the story had been stretched too far. Amongst the fossil fragments in Heather's office she also had the cricket bat out for us. As the story tells, this artificially shaped elephant bone tool found near the skull thought to ba a "ceremonial" object. What I had not appreciated from the images I had seen was how similar to the end of a cricket bat it really is. I had always pictured it as smaller, but it is not; it is almost exactly the right size. What a remarkable find, and since it is also a complete fake, what on earth was going through the mind of the faker when he placed this object to be found by Smith Woodward? Is it deliberately some kind of message? Is someone really trying to tell Smith Woodward that this whole thing is "wrong", a joke? Or is this just the faker running wild with his ideas?*

One of the authors at the Natural History Museum, holding the Piltdown cricket bat. Other Piltdown fragments are on the table.
© Andrew Shortland & Patrick Degryse.

"Sheffield Park Man" and tragedy

Back in 1915, *E. dawsoni* was at the height of its fame. The painting we have discussed was completed and no fewer than three books with Piltdown as a central element were published: *The Antiquity of Man* by Arthur Keith, *Diversions of a Naturalist* by Ray Lankester and *Ancient Hunters* by William Sollas (Professor of Geology at Oxford, and sometimes implicated in the Piltdown hoax). Not only that, but Dawson had some more luck in the gravels. In January 1915, he wrote to Smith Woodward, "I believe we are in luck again!" He had found two fragments of a further skull and, in July, a molar tooth, near Sheffield Park, a country house two miles from the Piltdown pit. However, just as with Barcombe Mills Man, the announcement of these finds was strangely muted. This time, though, there was at least one very definite reason – Dawson was ill. It is unclear when the illness started, but mid to late 1915 is probable. It is equally unclear what he was suffering from, although pernicious anaemia has been suggested. This is a rare illness caused by Vitamin B-12 deficiency, which leads to low red blood cell counts and a host of symptoms related to this, including weakness, tiredness, confusion and so on. He was confined to his house for rest through the Spring of 1916, but despite this, his condition worsened and he died on 10 August. He was only 52.

> *After our day of "mixed fortunes" at Piltdown – not getting in to see the monument and visiting a pub that was no long- er "The Piltdown Man" – we arrived at dusk in Lewes where Dawson had lived. His home, Castle Hill House, is a small prop- erty which is still there, on the High Street, near the Castle. We walked past his house, and then up around the Castle mound and down the other side to find the charmingly named church of St John Sub Castro. Behind the church is a burial ground, cared for, but rather dilapidated. Some of the monuments are in a poor state of repair, and when we were there the wall had*

collapsed, taking part of the gate with it. The burial ground was filled roughly in date order, and here Charles Dawson lies. His monument is a little knocked around, the cross is not straight, but at least it is still standing. It is inscribed:

In Loving Memory of
CHARLES DAWSON FSA
Who died 10th August 1916
Aged 52 years

Dawson's Grave in the St John Sub Castro churchyard,
Lewes, February 2019.
© Andrew Shortland & Patrick Degryse.

"FSA" stands for Fellow of the Society of Antiquaries, perhaps his proudest accolade. His wife Helene is commemorated below. She survived him by only a few months, dying in 1917. It is a small tragedy surrounded by graves that bear witness to the greater tragedy that was the cataclysm of the Great War. Standing there in the lonely churchyard, you are forcefully reminded that England was never the same again.

Sometime after Dawson's death, Smith Woodward was able to see the Sheffield Park Man fragments, now often termed "Piltdown II". He confirmed they were "well fossilised" and "stained brown with iron oxide in the usual manner". Exactly where they were found has been lost. However, the key point of this find was that once again ape-like teeth and a man-like skull had been found together. This was strong evidence against those who thought that the first *E. dawsoni* was a composite of two creatures – it could happen once by natural accident that these could be found together, but twice? Surely they had to be from one creature?

After Dawson's death, Smith Woodward went to some pains to recover the fragments of Barcombe Mills Man (subsequently often termed "Piltdown III", despite actually being found before Piltdown II). He wrote to Dawson's widow, specifically asking if he could examine all the skeletal material in her husband's collection prior to it being auctioned. The Piltdown III fragments were delivered to his office in January 1917 and they were accessioned into the BM(NH) collection, with a very brief description. However, he never published them, or wrote any formal report on them. Perhaps he thought that they were not quite as ancient as Dawson had believed?

More and more doubts – the next thirty years

Following Dawson's death, Smith Woodward continued his work at Piltdown. Indeed, on his retirement from the BM(NH) in 1924, he moved to Haywards Heath, less than ten miles from Piltdown. He continued regularly to work on the site for 21 years, but the results of this whole period are summed up in only one paragraph in *The Earliest Englishman* and the most significant part of that is only eight words: "We found nothing of interest in the gravel". Not a single fragment of hominid was found after Dawson's death, despite years of detailed searching.

Meanwhile, doubts as to the association of the skull and jaw continued to be expressed very directly, especially by American scholars such as Aleš Hrdlička and Gerrit Miller at the Smithsonian in Washington and William King Gregory at the American Museum of Natural History in New York. They were horrified by the reconstruction, believing that this "horrible monster" was undoubtedly two different species – a human skull associated with an ape jaw. This eventually crystallised into two camps: the "Monistic view", that one creature was involved, against the dualistic view that it was two. Debate raged over the twenties and early thirties. However, it was finds elsewhere that would cause the Piltdown supporters the most problems.

In 1924, workers in the Buxton Lime works, near Taung in South Africa, uncovered a very complete fossilised skull and jaw, which eventually found its way into the hands of Raymond Dart at the University of Witwatersrand. He identified it as a fossil ape with distinctly hominoid characteristics. Despite being small-brained, it had a jaw reminiscent of *H. Heidelbergensis* and nowhere near as ape-like as Piltdown, strongly suggesting that the ape stood erect. It became known as the "Taung Child" or, more formally, *Australopithecus africanus* – "Southern ape of Africa". More specimens were found in Sterkfontein, and then further hominids began to be found in Southern Africa, China and Palestine. All were significantly different from *E. Dawsoni* and yet consistent between themselves. *E. Dawsoni* began to look like some sort of offshoot of the main hominid line.

However, it was a further find in England that would be the catalyst for the unmasking of *E. Dawsoni*. On 29 June 1935, a Clapham dentist called Alvan Marston found a fragment of fossilised human skull in the gravels of the River Thames at Swanscombe in Kent, associated with undoubted flint tools of Acheulian type. Keith saw the skull and believed it to be a descendant of *E. Dawsoni* so more recent and more advanced. Smith Woodward was somewhat dismissive. Elliot Smith placed the Swanscombe skull as "more primitive" than *E. Dawsoni,* in direct contradiction. All involved were of the impression that the two skulls belonged to gravel terraces of roughly the same age. However, this changed dramatically when Kenneth Oakley, a geologist and palaeontologist in Smith Woodward's old Department at the BM(NH), pointed to new work that suggested the Piltdown gravels were much younger than previously thought, and *E. Dawsoni* was therefore much younger than the Swanscombe Man. The association of the ape-like jaw with such a young hominid began to look very unlikely.

The work was interrupted by another world war, during which, in 1944, Smith Woodward died, still in Sussex, still hunting. It is perhaps sometimes the case that the death of an individual will result in the reinterpretation of their work. Perhaps it is easier to question when the original author is no longer around. This certainly seems to be the case here, for Piltdown began to unravel with increasing speed. In 1947, Marston returned publicly to the fray to champion his Swanscombe fossil. At the Geologists Association's meeting in June 1947 he argued strongly that the Piltdown skull was relatively modern and not associated with the jaw. Furthermore, he repeated the claim made by Arthur Hopwood in the study of the Piltdown animal fossils, that Dawson had soaked his fossils in a "solution of bichromate of potash to harden them", hence changing their colour. However, it was the suggestion of Oakley at this meeting that was the most important. He suggested using the newly developed fluorine test to analyse the Piltdown finds to attempt to get a relative date.

The fluorine test

The test relied on trace levels of fluorine in groundwaters diffusing into bones that lay within the gravels or soils. The more fluorine in the bone the longer the bones had been in contact with the groundwater. The initial hope was that this could provide an absolute date for bones, but it was quickly realised that too many factors affected the rate of diffusion. However, it could be used to check whether bones had been in the soil for the same period of time – a relative date. Oakley managed to get permission from his own museum to conduct the analysis, which was carried out at the Government Laboratory in London in 1949. Oakley showed that the animal fossils of the Piltdown gravels had the expected high levels of fluorine, but *all* the *E. Dawsoni* fragments had very low levels. The jaw and the skull therefore seemed to belong together, but did not belong to the gravels in which they were found – perhaps they were washed in by a flood? Oakley believed that the Piltdown hominid fossils could be no older than "the last interglacial period", that is to say about 100,000 years, much younger than had been thought before. The fluorine test again suggested that *E. Dawsoni* was some sort of strange genetic throwback or side shoot, unrelated to the main trunk of human evolution and much more recent than many thought possible.

The bust

It was amongst all this doubt about the Piltdown finds that Joseph Weiner, an anthropologist at Oxford University, began to have his own doubts. Returning from a conference in which Piltdown had been raised, he was struck by the problems of the Piltdown assemblage. He recalled "thinking it over again, I realised with astonishment that while there were in fact only two possible 'natural' theories, i.e. that Piltdown man was in fact a man-ape of Woodward's interpretation, or that two distinct creatures, fossil man and fossil ape, had been found side by side, neither of the 'natural' explanations was at all satisfactory". Could the jaw be modern? But if it was then it was like no modern ape jaw, because the tooth wear was particularly man-like. "That would mean only one thing: deliberately ground-down teeth. Immediately this summoned up a devastating corollary – the equally deliberate placing of the jaw in the pit". Horrified and probably scared by his hypothesis, he consulted his boss, Professor Wilfred Le Gros Clarke, who was immediately convinced by the argument. Together they rang Oakley at the BM(NH) and asked, presumably extremely carefully, if there was any chance that the jaw could have been a fake. Oakley went away to look at the fossil, and then rang back the same day, "utterly convinced that artificial abrasion had been applied". Piltdown was a deliberate fake, "*E. Dawsoni* was not only dead; he had never lived".

The three men, Weiner, Le Gross Clark and Oakley, kept their findings secret and worked hard to prove their devastating hypothesis conclusively. However, as with a lot of other fakes and forgeries discussed in this book, as soon as the mind set had switched to doubting the object, it rapidly became clear that there were multiple issues with the fossils, all of which suggested deliberate forgery.

On 20 November 1953 they produced a paper that was taken up rapidly by the press. The work finally resulted in their publication of the key volume on Piltdown, *The Piltdown Forgery*. In it they showed clearly that many of the teeth of the jaw had been crudely filed down, with fine scratches still evident on some surfaces. The Piltdown canine, apparently so fortunately found that summer's day in 1913, had also been abraded to make it look more worn than it was, once again with visible scratches "which suggests the application of an abrasive".

❝ *Two interesting chance finds relate to the Piltdown story and work on the fossils by the three men at the University Museum at Oxford. The first I made at a bookshop in Hay-on-Wye, a small market town famous for having rather more secondhand bookshops than you would think a small town could support and a Mecca for the bibliophile. Browsing the shelves, I found a copy of Keith's book,* The Antiquity of Man, *in blue hardback, with a lovely Piltdown skull embossed in gold on the cover. I bought it for £5, but only when I got it home did I realise that it had an owner's name inside – "K.P. Oakley 5th August 1933". The book had been Oakley's own, bought just after he finished his first degree at University College London. He would have handled it and looked through it as he investigated the fraud and wrote his damning book.*

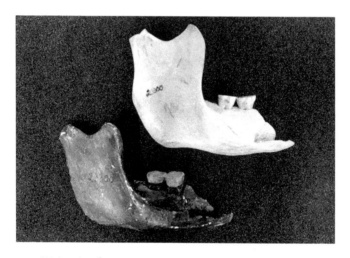

Weiner jaw from the University Museum, Oxford (top), with a stained cast of the original jaw specimen.
© Andrew Shortland & Patrick Degryse.

The second find was related to Weiner. I was paying a rare visit to the University Museum in Oxford, located in what is now the Science Area of the University of Oxford, I had spent my

41

undergraduate life next door in the Department of Geology. The University Museum is a smaller version of the BM(NH), with the same Neo-Gothic cathedral look. I was there looking through the anthropology collections when I happened to mention my longstanding interest in Piltdown Man. The Curator dived into a drawer and pulled out a fragment of jaw, identical to the Piltdown jaw in morphology, but unstained and very fresh. I had the chance to go back to the Museum in research for this book and met the Collections Manager for Zoology, Mark Carnall. He had been going through the Museum records for me and had turned up quite a lot of material, amongst which was the jaw. We studied it together and I suddenly realised where I had seen it before – it was depicted in Weiner's book where the authors exposed the fossils as fakes. On reading it again, it was clear what the University Museum still had – it was Weiner's 1950s attempt to replicate the fakery of the jaw, where he had used an ape jaw from the collection and replicated the breakages seen in the casts that he had of the original specimens. It was therefore a vital link in the chain of evidence that proved Piltdown was "wrong". Mark and I were delighted to work out what it was and to be able to give it its proper place in history.

In addition to the replica work, Weiner and team carried out a test of the organic content of the Piltdown fragments by measuring the nitrogen content of the bones. This was a relatively new method and showed that the jaw, canine and the molar (from Piltdown II) had nitrogen contents consistent with them being essentially modern. A review of the fluorine analysis and some new results found the same, with the cranium possibly being "Upper Pleistocene". Not only that, but the jaw and canine (at least) had been artificially stained, the canine by a "tough, flexible paint-like substance". The staining was tested at Oxford by a young, up-and-coming academic named Edward "Teddy" Hall. His new technique, X-Ray Fluorescence, showed that artificial paint had been applied to the surface of the finds. We shall encounter Teddy again when he appears in a pivotal role in the investigation of the Turin Shroud.

The conclusion was obvious. To use the words in *The Piltdown Hoax*, Piltdown was "a most elaborate and carefully planned hoax [...] and the perpetuation of the hoax appears to have been entirely unscrupulous and inexplicable, [with] no parallel in the history of palaeontological discovery". The obvious question remained, who did it?

The Perpetrator identified

Further work carried out by a range of authors showed that the Piltdown fragments were a collection of different species and ages: the jaw was that of an immature orang-utan and "entirely recent"; the canine tooth was painted with a modern paint, probably Vandyke brown and therefore modern; the flint implements were artificially stained and planted; the bone cricket bat had been shaped by a steel knife; the fauna was planted and some of it not from the UK. Finally, in 1959 the new technique of carbon dating was used on the cranium, which was known to be artificially stained, and the jaw.

Cranium from Piltdown I (GrN-2203)   620±100 BP
Jaw from Piltdown I (GrN2204)   500±100 BP

The equivalent dates for these were 1210-1480 CE and 1290-1640 CE, so they were likely to be more or less contemporaneous and medieval in date. However, the jaw was dated again in the late 1980s by the latest AMS-based radiocarbon technique (see Turin Shroud for more details on this technique). The date for the jaw was different:

Jaw from Piltdown I (OxA-1395)   90±120 BP

This is essentially a modern date – 1630-1950 CE. The difference in the two dates is an oddity that has not been explained, but may be down to contamination in the first sample. A nineteenth century date for the orang-utan jaw would fit very well with the perpetrator obtaining a jaw from a museum or private collection, whereas the earlier date is somewhat harder to understand.

Over the years since the unveiling of the fraud, many, many individuals have been accused of being implicated in it. As Miles Russell says, "attempting to wade through and assess each and every accusation can be a laborious and unrewarding task". It seems that some of the accusations have been made largely on the grounds of attempting to sell books – the evidence against them is at best ephemeral, at worst non-existent. Thus names such as Sir Arthur Conan Doyle, William Sollas and a host of minor players have all been suggested; quite why is not clear to us. However, there are a group of suspects, all of whom gained from the association with Piltdown, who are at least worth a passing glance. Let us first consider the central figure in the Painting. Seated in the white laboratory coat is Sir Arthur Keith, knighted for his services to science, author of *The Antiquity of Man* with that profile of *E. Dawsoni* embossed in gold on its hard cover. Spencer firmly points the finger at Keith in his 1990 book, but his evidence seems to consist largely in the fact that Keith, questioned forty years after the events, found it difficult to recall some of the detail. Besides, Keith was not present on the site when the fossil fragments were found. Could he have sneaked in, salted the gravels, and left? What are the chances of the excavators finding the small fragments he hid? Surely the person who carried out the fraud had to be present at the time the bones were found. Thus others in the Painting can be dismissed in the same way. For example, Sir Grafton Elliot Smith was never present and had no regular access to the site, which would have been required to carry this out.

Father Teilhard de Chardin was present for some of the excavations. He rose to be an eminent academic anthropologist, was cited for bravery for his service as a stretcher-bearer in World War I and travelled widely in China, Africa and throughout Asia. The case against Teilhard de Chardin concerns the motive for the hoax. The idea that the hoax was a joke that went wrong has been used as a motive for a number of suspects. It started as a simple piece of fun, but got completely out of hand and then was impossible to stop or reveal. The idea is that the French Teilhard de Chardin is playing a joke on his English friends because England had such a poor hominid fossil record. What better joke for a Frenchman than to place in the hands of the "earliest Englishman" a tool that resembled nothing greater than a broken cricket bat? However, amusing though it is, there are terminal problems in suggesting that Teilhard de Chardin was the hoaxer, the most important of which is that he was not even in the country when some of the important fragments were found – he could not possibly have planted them.

This leaves two individuals who undoubtedly were on site when the finds were made, and both gained hugely from association with Piltdown – Smith Woodward and Dawson. Smith Woodward certainly had the expertise to carry out the scientific aspects of the hoax. Weiner, Oakley and Le Gros Clarke, despite their extensive scientific work on the Piltdown fragments, do not name a perpetrator. They explore many of the options for the hoax, the motives and the practicalities, but they do not come to a conclusion. Weiner, Oakley and Le Gros Clarke might well draw back from accusing a distinguished previous Keeper at the BM(NH) and one of Oakley's predecessors. Smith Woodward certainly did not ask Dawson some hard questions as to how the fragments were found, and the note-taking on site was apparently non-existent. However, would a hoaxer, in retirement, move to a house just down the road from the site and spend the next twenty years of his life desperately searching for more evidence? Twenty years to find "nothing of interest in the gravel". This is surely not the action of the hoaxer. Undoubtedly, Smith Woodward believed Dawson too much and should have asked him a whole range of searching questions, but his only crime is his gullibility.

This leaves us with the Uckfield solicitor, Charles Dawson. The usual defence of Dawson is that he did not have the skills to fool the leading scientists in the UK and eventually the world. Not only that, but he was a "thoroughly honest man", "too honest and faithful to his research". Surely he was an "innocent victim". He was, however, at the very centre of this, the instigator and present when all the finds were made. There is another piece of evidence too, which was turned up by Weiner whilst he was interviewing people connected with Piltdown for his book. He heard that an earlier collector and archaeologist, called Harry Morris, had thought that the "stone tools" found in the Piltdown I dig were faked. He apparently had one of them, somehow, and had written that it was "wrong". Morris had since died, but his cabinet of fossils had been bequeathed to his friend, A. P. Morris. Unfortunately, Morris was not interested in fossils and had (as the story gets more and more curious) "swapped it" for a collection of birds' eggs with a Frederick Wood. Wood died shortly afterwards, but Weiner traced his wife, who still had the cabinet. In it was the Piltdown flint, on the surface of which Morris had written, "Stained by C. Dawson with intent to defraud (all)– H.M.". On a piece of paper with it he had written, "Stained with permanganate of potash and exchanged by D. for my most valued specimen! – H.M.". A third note said:

> "Judging from an overheard conversation there is every reason to suppose that the canine tooth found at Pdown was imported from France! I challenge SK Museum authorities to test the implements of the same patina as this stone which the imposter Dawson says were 'excavated from the Pit'! They will be found [to] be white if hydrochlorate acid be applied – H.M. Truth will out".

SK Museum is South Kensington Museum, or the BM(NH); hydrochlorate should be hydrochloric. Various lines of evidence suggest that at least some of the notes were written in Dawson's lifetime, so before 1916. The most important point seems to be that Morris is complaining about Dawson faking an item using the same sort of staining that was used on the skull and jaw – he not only had the ability to do it, he had done it.

However there is another line of argument that can be used with Dawson. Miles Russell conducted a survey of Dawson's other work and published it in his marvellous book, *Piltdown Man: the secret life of Charles Dawson*. What Russell shows very clearly is that Piltdown Man was not the only hoax that Dawson was involved in; there were many. A considerable number of objects which were associated with him, and he had gifted to museums, found, described or otherwise been involved with, were not what they were made out to be. This range of objects included bronzes, bricks, flints, images on walls, a boat, statues, fossils, bones, sites and went as far as the truly bizarre – a live toad found encased within a void in stone. Russell accounts for at least 33 clear fakes for which "the chief (and sometimes *only*) suspect ... is none other than Charles Dawson himself. Dawson was without doubt creating fakes on a grand scale, and passing them off to colleagues, museums and academic journals. It seems beyond reasonable doubt that the Piltdown hoaxes were part of this, and were created by this quiet, unassuming, small town solicitor".

The hoax was to cause British palaeoanthropology much wasted work and much embarrassment over the years. However, it is worth returning to where we started, to Arthur Smith Woodward. It is curious that while, as discussed above, many individuals in the Painting wrote books about or including *Eoanthropus dawsoni*, Smith Woodward's book is interestingly different from the others. Firstly, it was not published at the time of the discovery when Piltdown was all over the press. The first chapter was written, but it was "laid aside for more immediate technical work", according to the Prefactory Note in the book, written by his wife, Maud. The Note says that Smith Woodward had gone blind in late life, and finishing this book was given as a task by his wife to "give him occupation ... and bring a degree of happiness", "The last word was written the day before he died". Sir Arthur Keith wrote the foreword and is thanked by Maud as an "old and much valued friend" – apparently early tiffs about the reconstruction of *Eoanthropus* long forgotten. The book is also very small, less than 17cm high, the size of a small pocket notebook and only 120 or so pages – half the size and a third the thickness of Keith's *The Antiquity of Man*. The first words of Chapter 1, the only one that Maud tells us was written at the time, are "Charles Dawson…". The first paragraph describes Dawson's huge range of interests, even including the "live toad in stone". The book is a tribute to Dawson, both from Smith Woodward and from Keith. As such it is rather a sad little book. Both Smith Woodward and Keith remain convinced to the last about *Eoanthropus* and Dawson. Indeed Keith says:

> "In these pages Smith Woodward does Dawson full justice. My heart went out to Dawson, the scholarly solicitor; as long as England can produce such men, her place in the Society of Nations is assured".

In a final note, when one visits UK museums, because many are such longstanding institutions, curators can sometimes casually mention things that they have come across that you did not know about. Small twists in the story that seem insignificant to them, but have a wider interest to the investigator. Some museums, as mentioned above, have unaccessioned material that was pushed into cupboards a hundred years ago and modern curators, with huge time pressures to teach, publish and conserve, have only limited resources to investigate.

One of these moments happened at the Oxford University Museum with Mark Carnall. He openly admitted that "in honour of my visit" he had looked through some of the cupboards and found boxes labelled "Piltdown" that he had never had time to open. Such statements always send a frisson of excitement down the spine of the investigator – what could be in there? In the end the boxes contained teaching and display casts of the Piltdown finds that had been used, presumably in the 1920s when the fos-

sils were still the most exciting thing in British palaeoanthropology. However, in the last box there was a peculiar white lump, somewhat smaller than a skull, and curiously knobbly. We recognised it immediately, although I had never seen one "in the flesh" before – it was the endocast from the Piltdown painting – the curious white object on the table, plumb centre, in front of Arthur Keith in his white labcoat. To my knowledge, it is the only one to have survived of what must have been a very limited run of casts. Mark is now curating all this teaching material as, although not "real fossils", even casts obviously have an important part in the history of our understanding of those fossils and the development of the subject.

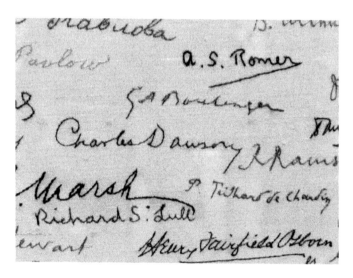

Charles Dawson's signature (with "P. Teilhard de Chardin"), embroidered by Mrs Smith Woodward, on the Smith Woodward Tablecloth, now in the Natural History Museum.
© Andrew Shortland & Patrick Degryse.

There was a second, even more remarkable moment at the BM(NH). We were just leaving and chatting generally to Heather, when she said, "Oh, I nearly forgot, would you like to see the tablecloth?". There is only one possible reaction to that, and Patrick and I spoke it in unison, "What tablecloth?". Heather led us along dimly lit corridors, up and down stairs, past case after case of specimens to a nondescript corridor near some curators' offices in the non-public area of the museum. There on the wall, mounted in a glass case, was a 120cm square tablecloth with a display card beside it naming it as "The Smith Woodward Tablecloth". It seems that Mrs Smith Woodward had developed a "novel hostess custom" that when they had a distinguished visitor to tea at the Smith Woodward house, she would ask them to sign the tablecloth and then, later, would embroider over their signature to preserve it – zoologists, botanists, geologists and palaeontologists, each subject with its own corner of the cloth. 342 signatures are now present, including giants of the scientific world like Raymond Dart (who found Australopithecus, *discussed above), Marie Stopes (a palaeobotanist, better known for pioneering birth control) along with Pierre Teilhard de Chardin and Arthur Smith Woodward himself, much discussed here. Of course, there was only one name we hunted for. He was there, in his neat solicitor's script in the heart of all these distinguished academic names: Charles Dawson.*

Chapter 3
The Getty Kouros

Visiting "The Getty" is always an experience. While other American museums are quite obviously wealthy and unafraid of showing it, the Getty sets a new height for display and confidence. Perhaps this is in part due to its setting, on the edge of Los Angeles, adjacent to Hollywood. We were always happy to visit colleagues there and there was always an added frisson, for sitting on the edge of Tinseltown, overlooking the smog and (sometimes) the City, the Getty is the wealthiest museum in the World.

The Getty is a conglomerate of institutes and laboratories, strangely intertwined for historical (and probably tax) reasons. Currently the overarching J. Paul Getty Trust is the world's largest cultural and philanthropic organisation dedicated to the visual arts and it funds four institutes: The Getty Conservation Institute is interested in all aspect of cultural heritage conservation; The Getty Foundation is the grant-awarding side, supporting visual arts widely; The J. Paul Getty Museum "collects, presents, conserves, and interprets great works of art"; and, finally, The Getty Research Institute carries out research in art history and related areas.

"The Getty" started out at the grace of John Paul Getty, an entrepreneur-billionaire who made his fortune in oil. He had a keen interest in art, calling it one of the "few lasting products of human endeavor", but also saw it as a personal addiction, one he could not quit though it conflicted with his renowned stinginess – he was extraordinarily careful with money. So while on one hand he was spending millions on art and antiques, he was also religiously recording personal expenditure, literally down to the last cent, in a notebook he carried with him. His collecting did not focus on a specific period or material and it seems that he was not thinking of a coherent collection. Some collectors are driven by a period, civilisation, artist or material (paintings, glass, porcelain, etc.), but Getty acquired all that caught his eye and became available on the market. He was a bargain hunter, who started collecting just after the Great Depression, looking for undervalued art or cheap offers, especially in Europe just before the Second World War. If any area appealed to him most, it would probably be Ancient Greek and Roman art, as though this somehow offered him a way back into time. A student of ancient history, he often visited archaeological sites and saw himself as the modern equivalent of the Roman emperor Hadrian: an educated traveller and patron of the arts.

The Getty Villa, where the Kouros was studied and displayed.
© Andrew Shortland & Patrick Degryse.

Getty amassed such a great number of art objects that they would no longer fit into his comparatively modest Malibu home, a ranch in a canyon off the Pacific Coast Highway. He began giving away objects in return for tax write-offs, but his accountant soon suggested the creation of his own non-profit-making museum. In this way he could keep the art and the tax advantage – this is the sort of deal that was guaranteed to appeal to Getty. The J. Paul Getty Museum therefore saw the light of day in December 1953 in the form of five small galleries and an art library. It was too small to contain all the objects, so some of the larger objects were kept outside in the courtyard. The museum had virtually no opening hours, only 3pm to 5pm on Wednesdays and Fridays, just enough to be "charitable" and therefore tax-exempt. It had only 24 parking spaces, which had to be booked in advance, unheard of in a state where everyone drives everywhere. By the late 1960s, major remodelling was necessary, and in 1970 it was decided a new building would be constructed. This became the somewhat controversial modern copy of the ancient Roman *Villa dei Papiri* in Pompeii, just outside Naples, the original of which was buried by the eruption of Vesuvius in 79 CE and subsequently excavated in the eighteenth century. In January 1974, this new Getty Museum, now known as the Getty Villa, opened. Though widely criticised around the world as a tasteless amusement park ("Kitsch city" or "Plastic Paradise", both comments from the *Los Angeles Times*), the public loved "Pompeii-on-the-Pacific" and came to see the building more than the art in it. However, staff at the museum were discontented with the lack of really high-quality art on display. They had to almost beg for purchases, but Getty refused to use his wealth to acquire top artefacts or to compete for masterpieces – he bought what he wanted, not what his élite, academic, employees wanted. This rather rapidly changed when, upon his death in 1976, Getty bequeathed most of his fortune to his small museum in Malibu. Overnight it became the richest private art enterprise in the World.

Feeling an urgent need to place itself in the field and to become not only the wealthiest, but also a most spectacular collection, the J. Paul Getty Museum was now ready to spend its "inheritance" to acquire some really prize antiquities. Indeed, for tax purposes, it actually had to spend the considerable sums accrued in interest or face losing charitable tax advantages. While J. Paul Getty himself was

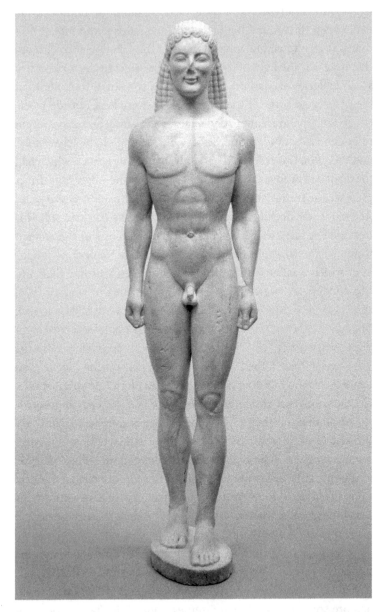

The Getty Kouros.
Digital image courtesy of the Getty's Open Content Program.

by instinct careful and cautious and had always wanted assurances on the legal status of objects, sometimes with money-back guarantees, the Museum perhaps had a more "flexible" attitude to these matters. The origin or legal status of possible purchases mattered, but the desire to have the best objects was paramount and, with the money of the J. Paul Getty Museum Trust, the means were there to do this. It now became a matter of seizing the right opportunities.

One such unique chance occurred in 1983, when a wonderful example of a late archaic Greek marble kouros sculpture appeared on the art market. A "kouros" (plural, "kouroi") is a large statue of a standing, single figure of a naked youth. Up to three metres tall, with the left foot slightly advanced in a vaguely Egyptian fashion, they are usually of marble, but can occasionally be in other stone and other materials. Kouroi date from the late seventh to the sixth centuries BCE, but what they were used for is not really known, although they may be linked to the God Apollo. They are rare, the Getty one possibly being one of only twelve remaining complete statues, making the sale of such a well-preserved example extraordinary indeed. It was offered by the Switzerland-based art dealer Gianfranco Becchina (who had supplied a number of pieces to the Getty) to the then Getty curator of antiquities, Jiri Frel. Frel had previously worked at the Metropolitan Museum of Art, New York ("The Met"), and before that as a professor at Charles University in Prague. As a refugee from his home country of Czechoslovakia, Frel was a survivor with a natural disregard for the detail of rules. He was an immensely talented man: he spoke six languages, played the violin and had a weakness for wearing sandals over socks. Friends said of him that "he loved food, women, everything" and "was a real bon vivant". He was married at least three times, and had something of a reputation in the institutions in which he worked. The best picture of him shows him sitting in one of the exhibition rooms of the Getty Villa in front of his favourite object, a bronze statue known as *Victorious Youth,* for which he had negotiated the purchase for the Museum after Getty's death. In the picture (without sandals) Frel looks completely relaxed and supremely confident, the alpha male in his own territory. He was the sort of character who just knew he was right – an absolute belief in his own ability – and this was going to cause him, and even more so The Getty, a good deal of trouble.

As any museum would do, The Getty wanted to know where the Kouros had come from. Becchina did what dealers would do and duly provided documents detailing the history, the "provenance" of the piece. The documents traced the piece to Switzerland, more specifically to a collector in Geneva, who in 1930 had purchased it from a Greek dealer. Here the trail ran cold. Before this date, there was no evidence of its history, although that was by no means unusual. The Getty wanted a closer look at the sculpture, so it was agreed that it would be brought to Malibu along with the various provenance documents supporting the piece's authenticity and legal status. In December 1983, it was viewed by the Trustees of the Museum in the Getty's conservation laboratories. Such a high-value piece would have to have the agreement of the Trustees in order for it to be purchased, so this was an important step. Unfortunately, it immediately caused controversy. Frederico Zeri, a founder trustee of the Museum and something of a "fake buster", immediately called it an "incredible joke". He said it was "Marvellous. Extremely complex", "but it is clearly a fake". He and other scholars were unhappy with many aspects of the piece, ranging from flaws in the stone of the forehead to the way the fingernails were portrayed. Others pointed to the eclectic style, displaying stylistic features that usually occur wide apart in time. So there were many negative opinions. However, while

The Victorious Youth,
from the Getty collection,
but claimed by Italy.

Digital image courtesy of the
Getty's Open Content Program.

the eclectic style would be exceptional, it is not impossible for such kouroi, and with so few examples known, even a stylistically odd one was still possible. The problem for stylistic experts was that the twelve kouroi known were also all different, so the Kouros on offer to The Getty was not exceptional in this way. If it fell further from the norm than usual, could it not just be a later (or earlier) piece? Or a different artist, a contemporary copy, or have a different, special function, now unknown, that meant it had to be different? If you wanted to believe in it, and Frel really did, then there were a myriad of reasons for why the statue might be "right".

However, the museum had another worry about the piece. Yes, it might be fake, but if it was not, then could it be looted? The paperwork stopped in 1930 and so no find site was recorded. This was worrying, and although Frel thought that it might have been taken by a notorious looter in the 1930s, too long ago to make it easy for a country to claim it back, the possibility that it was looted later than this was a nagging problem. Only the all-important provenance paperwork showed that it had been "out of the ground" in the middle of the twentieth century. Looting was a real issue in the 1980s, as it still is in many areas of the World today. However, in the 1980s the problem was much more widespread and fuelled by the attitude of some auction houses and major museums. It was widely known at the time that the majority of objects on the antiquities market were recently excavated in Greece or Italy and illegally exported, having been smuggled across borders. A Getty curator wrote that "95% of the antiquities on the market have been found in the last three years". Switzerland, and especially the cities of Zurich and Geneva, was a node through which pieces were "laundered", giving them new owners and new provenances. Not that some of the museums seemed to care that much. Some Getty curators themselves adopted a simple procedure known as "optical due diligence". The idea of this was to look through the paperwork connected with an object to give the appearance that an object's background had been carefully checked. However, the paperwork would not be rigorously questioned, but taken at face value. This way, dates, people or signatures would be taken for what they were rather than taking easy steps to check catalogues and ring contacts to ensure independent verification of the documents. The idea was deliberately to avoid "certain knowledge" that the object was looted – do not look too carefully, or too deeply. The Getty was far from alone in this; in fact its acquisition policy was on a par with those of some other major US museums. In addition to this, the actual legal situation was uncertain, with the UNESCO convention, requiring an object under sale to have provenance reaching to before 1970, entering American law only in the same year, 1983. This meant that it had yet to be properly tested, and The Getty, being hugely wealthy, could afford the very best lawyers if it needed them. This was a pretty widespread attitude at the time. Even the ultra-strict, very ethically aware Harvard Fogg Museum required only "reasonable reassurance" that the object had been out of its country of origin before 1970. The Met did not require documents, and even the Boston Museum of Fine Art was prepared simply to take a dealer's word on the provenance. However, the academic archaeologists of the Archaeological Institute of America were scathing. They pushed, and continue to push, for a no tolerance attitude to looting and collecting. This matter caused a serious rift between university and museum academics, who might well have trained in the same classes and the same universities, but ended up defending very different ethical positions on the possession of antiquities.

However, such a light touch system was already causing problems. The Met was fighting its own battle over a piece as the debate over the Kouros went on. In 1972, it had bought a Greek, red-figure krater (a large open mouthed vase) from Robert Hecht, an American dealer with excellent connections in Italy, Greece and Turkey. This spectacular piece was the only surviving work of the painter Euphronios and depicted youths arming for battle and a scene from the Trojan wars. So special was the vase that The Met paid a world record price of $1 million. There was no doubt that the piece was genuine, but dark rumours were circulating that it had been recently excavated from an Etruscan Tomb near Cervetti.

American museums buying material that had highly problematic origins put the museums and the academic archaeological community at loggerheads and created rifts that have yet to heal. The Archaeological Institute of America described the Getty's purchasing strategies as "wholly unacceptable", and stated that they compromised all who came into contact with them. For an archaeologist, the context of the piece, the way it interrelates to other pieces it is found with, its find site and the sites around are all invaluable sources of evidence that help to reconstruct an ancient world, and these are immediately lost if an object is merely dug up, taken and sold. On the other hand, the museums felt they had a responsibility to acquire, protect and preserve objects, to study and publish them for all scholars to see. Their argument was that buying the objects might save them from being lost or destroyed. However, they did at least privately admit to the key point that the archaeologists were making: buying the objects creates a market which encourages more objects to be looted.

The Kouros was bought by the J. Paul Getty Museum in 1985 for another record of $9.5 million dollars, and first exhibited in October 1986.

"My first trip to Los Angeles occurred soon after the Kouros first went on display. I was completing a World tour and flew in to LA from Hawaii. I can still remember the first sight of the city – an endless grid of low rise housing stretching out into the smog. It seemed to go on forever. The Getty Museum was one of the places I really wanted to see but, as with all visitors even then, I had to get out to the Villa, some miles up the PCH. Feeling like the only man in LA over 20 who could not drive, I remember taking a rare bus and doing quite a lot of walking. The Villa was striking, like nothing else in LA, and a real ocean of calm. I remember it also being almost deserted (unlike on many later visits) and wandering out into the gardens. The "Roman villa" really appeared to sit alone on the hillside surrounded by scrub. I do not remember many of the pieces in the collection, but

the Kouros stands out clearly. It is a very impressive piece, slightly over life size, but appearing taller than that. And it did remind me very much of some Egyptian pieces. The quite Egyptian formalised stance, the clenched fists and the distant look in the eyes all recalled Pharaonic statues to me. The nature of the carving, especially of the body, was much more Greek. At the time, I was merely admiring as a tourist the latest acquisition of a World famous museum, and did not know that I would see it again and again, and that it would go on to be a source of such controversy.

Curator Jiri Frel was not around to see it exhibited. In addition to his work on bringing key pieces into the Museum, since J. Paul Getty's death Frel had been trying to build a unique study collection. He envied the excavated collections of the great East Coast museums. These museums, with their Ivy League credentials and collaborators, had been involved in excavating some of the World's key archaeological sites. This resulted in excavated material which the museums could display, but also in large quantities of sherds and other broken material which would never be suitable for display. However, what these collections did do was attract academics to study and publish them. From an academic point of view, such excavated collections were at least as important as, if not more so than, single, high-prestige pieces. These collections attracted scholars from throughout the World to visit and study. The scholars interacted with the curators, who acted as "gate keepers" to the material, and wrote up their findings with the curators as co-authors on their papers. Frel wanted to be part of this élite international network, and while the headline objects brought in the public, it was the study collection that attracted the scholars. The Getty Board would not pay for minor pieces; they were interested only in the very biggest, the oldest, the best. So Frel came up with a scheme that would create his desired collection – he would get people to give it to him. This is not as crazy as it sounds, as in America people giving gifts to charitable organisations such as museums can claim back a certain percentage of their value in tax breaks, and regularly do so. This is what makes

American museums and, perhaps even more so their universities, the wealthiest in the world and the envy of their relatively impoverished European equivalents. There is nothing wrong, and everything right, with this system. However, Frel was to take this model several stages further and create a whole world of trouble. He quickly realised that the value of an object (and therefore the amount of tax relief) was determined by expert opinion, and this was the weakness that he exploited. He approached owners and asked for the gift of something that they had paid say $10,000 for. However, he valued it at perhaps $50,000 when it came to the Museum. This way the Getty was getting what were apparently very high-value gifts, which reflected very well on Frel with the Trustees, who praised his amazing ability to talk people into giving to the Museum. Even better, the owners were making more money in tax breaks than they had actually paid for the piece (the tax break on $50,000 being more than the original cost price of $10,000). Thus both the owner and the Museum gained; only the poor American taxpayer lost out. Over several years this became a crazy scheme. Sometimes the "owners" never even saw the piece, Frel selected the object, bought it for the museum with the owners' money, faked the valuations, and gave the object to the Museum. Once again the owners made more money in tax breaks than they had originally donated to the Museum, and Frel got exactly the relatively low-value study collections he was craving. The sums became enormous – typical of figures towards the end of the scheme included an owner paying $75,000 for an object for the museum which Frel then valued at $2.5 million, earning the owner $1.2 million in tax breaks. It was true Hollywood – Frel got his study collection and a lot of people made a lot of money for doing nothing. What could possibly go wrong? Dozens of people were involved when the scheme was shut down by the IRS and the Getty quietly sent Frel "on sabbatical" to Italy. He never returned.

Soon after the Kouros' unveiling things started to unravel openly for the Getty and its new acquisition. "Optical due diligence" of the provenance documents had been sufficient for the Getty to buy the sculpture. However, a closer look had revealed, as some of the curators had perhaps always quietly suspected, that the paperwork accompanying the object was highly suspicious. As the curators began to unpack the details, it became frankly disturbing. The papers reconstructed a timeline for the object, when it was where and who had seen it. This revealed that it had come to the attention of some key scholars of the period. Obviously, an early dated letter that mentioned the Kouros showed that the object had been around then and that it had not been relatively recently either made or looted. It was a bonus if the letter was written by a great scholar who stated that they approved of it. A letter dated 1952 did exactly this. It was from a pre-eminent scholar of Greek sculpture, Ernst Langlotz, Professor at the University of Bonn and Director of the Akademisches Kunstmuseum there until his retirement in 1963. He remarked on the similarity of the Kouros to other known authentic sculptures of the time. However, later inquiries by the Getty revealed that the postcode on the letter did not exist until twenty years after the date of the letter. Furthermore, Professor Langlotz had written a second letter vouching for another piece that the Getty had bought. Comparing the signatures of the two letters, they were completely different. One, or more likely both, were fakes – Professor Langlotz died in 1978 so was not around to comment on or contradict the letters. Another letter discussing repairs to the statue made in 1955 mentioned a bank account that was not opened until 1963. The provenance history of the sculpture was evidently an elaborate, if not too careful, fake. This meant that there was effectively no provenance for the statue before its sudden appearance on the art market in 1983. The fake documents were there to create a history and therefore presumably deliberately hide its very recent source. But this did not really help to decide if the statue was genuine or not. Whether the statue was fake or looted, both scenarios would require a provenance, a "legend", to (at least superficially) cover the tracks of the faker/looter. In fact, the rather poor quality of the provenance documents, always suspected by some of those closely connected with the Kouros, might hint at the option that the object was genuine. After all, why waste time on this aspect when "optical due diligence" was all that was required for a genuine object? A superficial, authentic-looking series of documents might be all that was needed in this case.

So the Kouros appears suddenly in 1983, but still could be genuine or fake. In terms of a date, it is therefore very likely to be either from the sixth century BCE or the twentieth century CE. It is vanishingly unlikely to be anything in between. This is quite a date range and, at first glance, seems to offer a real possibility to determine which is more likely. So what techniques can be used to date a marble statue?

The first technique has not changed in hundreds (perhaps thousands) of years. To determine the age of a marble statue, that is to say when exactly it was carved and hence vouch for its authenticity, the main technique is still based on the connoisseur's eye. Stylistic dating looks at the way the artist worked the stone, how the image was portrayed and whether the specific features of the sculpture belong to the time and style period it is said to belong to. Art historians will argue that there are stylistic reasons to believe that a stone object does or does not belong to a specific school, style or time period, as happened in the early conference at the Getty on the Kouros, discussed later in this chapter. The "eye" is really a very personal opinion, based upon expertise and knowledge of similar objects to compare to. Sometimes a connoisseur will not even be sure why they do not "like" an object and can find it difficult to describe. However, they are often right. Their experience based on seeing many similar objects and having an innate feeling for the material type and the period can be very revealing. But, of course, it remains in essence a subjective opinion and can leave much room for debate. As mentioned before, this is especially true when, as in the case of the Kouros, there are few comparanda to work from. In addition, as will be pointed out again and again in this book, experts are only human and have desires and wishes which they consciously or unconsciously hold. Often they may really *want* an object to be right, either because they are a curator and the object will be in their museum, or because they just want to be associated with finding a spectacular new object, valuable both monetarily and historically. This desire can influence an opinion without it even being obvious to the person expressing it. Not only that, but when one really desires an object to be the real thing, such debates become not only heated, but also tainted with personal sentiments. Thus each side, right or wrong, ends up "digging in" with its opinion and the normal academic debate over whether the object is real can almost cease. This is especially true if lawyers become involved, or are threatened to be involved. It is clear that another, independent approach is needed. Thus, once again, science comes to be relied upon to give an opinion.

> *My first time travelling to Los Angeles and the Getty left an impression that is still fresh in my mind. Not only was it my first 12-hour flight with associated jetlag, but also introductions to LAX, Santa Monica lifeguards and plastic surgery commercials are quite memorable. Going through the galleries of the Getty Villa for a first introduction, I was led, not coincidentally, to the kouros. It was at a moment when the conservation scientists there were looking into the sculpture again, to see if they could push knowledge of it somewhat further, even if only marginally. My brain was picked for what advances in stone research had been made over the last years, if any new approaches and methods had appeared, and if anything original could be done. This is a recurring process – every decade or so, and to this day, debated objects are held under the microscope again, sometimes literally, to see if, with the passing of time and progress of research and science, anything new can be found on the same material.*

The first stage of any scientific, analytical approach to ancient objects is to determine the material used to make the object. Here, the stone type would be obvious to any undergraduate geology student in their first year – marble is common and easily identified. However, this immediately causes us problems. Since it is so common, how can we tell whether this marble came from an ancient quarry in the right area for the making of kouroi, or from a completely nonsensical quarry that opened in the twentieth century and is hundreds of miles away? Marble varies to a limited extent in terms of its detailed structural, mineralogical and chemical characteristics. Occasionally these are helpful, but often not. One important characteristic of the Kouros marble was that it was relatively rich in the mineral dolomite. Marble is made up of carbonate minerals, essentially calcite (calcium carbonate) and dolomite (calcium magnesium carbonate). The Kouros marble is "dolomitic", so the bulk of the stone has significant amounts of the magnesium-rich mineral in it. This is an important criterion, which will be discussed later. There is another important variation that can be used to determine the source of ancient marbles, and this is linked once again to the mineral component of the stone. The two carbonate minerals, calcite and dolomite, contain abundant carbon and oxygen. As discussed elsewhere in this book, many elements, including carbon and oxygen, exist in different forms known as isotopes. These are variants of the element that have slightly different mass due to different numbers of neutrons in the nuclei of the atoms. Because they are different masses, the different isotopes of the same element act slightly differently in chemical processes. This tends to concentrate either the heavier or lighter isotope over the other one, hence the ratio of one isotope to the other changes – often only very slightly, but enough to measure. Through geological time, processes such as exposure to high pressure and temperature at depth in the earth subtly change the ratios of the carbon and oxygen isotopes in marbles in different regions in different ways. This allows marbles from different areas to be distinguished on the basis of differing isotopic ratios. Quarries providing stone from geological resources reflect those ratios and carry them on into the stone they produce. Over four or more decades archaeologists have attempted to track down all the sources of marble in the Eastern Mediterranean and scientists have characterised the carbon and oxygen isotopic ratios for them. In this way there is a database of marble isotopic (and other chemical) compositions to compare an analysis from the Kouros with, which can say from which quarry or geological region the marble it is made from might have originated. The question to be answered then becomes whether the stone used originates from a plausible source, such as a quarry that was active during the time the statue was supposedly carved, or a problematic source, for example a modern quarry.

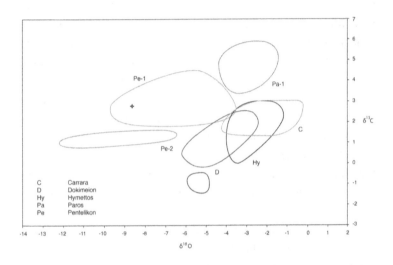

A typical diagram comparing the oxygen-carbon stable isotopic composition of marble quarries to that of a sample from an ancient statue (indicated by the star). In this case, the ancient statue is consistent with an origin from certain marble quarries in Penteli, Greece.
Data and © Andrew Shortland & Patrick Degryse.

Of course, life is never that simple – there are some restrictions on this work. The major one is that the isotopic fingerprint of a number of quarries is not unique, but overlaps with those of other quarries. This means that some quarries cannot be separated from each other – they have almost identical characteristics. Equally, it is possible that not all the quarries used in the past have been found – there could be more out there that simply have not been identified, and which may also have similar isotopic fingerprints. However, when a sample of the Getty Kouros was analysed, the fact that it was made from a *dolomitic* marble, combined with its stable isotope characteristics, meant that it could only really come from one quarry region, on the island of Thasos at the Northern end of the Aegean Sea. This is a correct material for the time and region, it is "consistent with the ancient date" as scientists would phrase it. However, again, such evidence is not absolute. Even though the correct stone source was used for the sculpture, this does not mean that the object was sculpted in a particular time period. It is perfectly possible, as long as a source is not exhausted, for a knowledgeable forger to take stone from the correct quarry and use that particular source. The Thasos quarries are huge and indeed still active. You can still buy statues, tiles or random blocks of stone of Thasian marble freely on the internet. The stone type used does not show that the Kouros is ancient or modern, real or fake, but it does show that if it is a fake the forger took care to use a stone that was consistent with the period. Further stages of analysis are therefore necessary, and it is at this point that it becomes particularly difficult to find an appropriate scientific approach.

Absolute dating of the statue by scientific means to give a calendrical date when it was made would, of course, be hugely useful. Absolute dating techniques will be discussed more in the chapter on the Turin Shroud, as their application there was intensely debated, and such methods would have been very useful on the Piltdown skull as well. However, absolute dating is extremely difficult in this particular case. The problem is that the date needed is when the stone was *carved*, not when it was *formed*. It is often possible, if the correct sample could be taken, to date when the *rock* itself was *formed*. This is a standard geological technique used throughout the world by geochronologists and relies on radioactive decay of elements such as rubidium or uranium. However, a date for the formation of the rock of a stone object statue would not be of much use (except perhaps if you were interested in provenancing the stone to a quarry). The stone will have a geological age tens or hundreds of millions of years older than the moment when the rock was *carved* into an object, and the carving process will not change that date. So in the case of the Kouros it takes us no further. What is needed is a date for the carving of the stone, not of the stone itself, and obtaining such a date is possible only in rare cases. Probably our one chance is to study the patina on the object. Patina is the corrosion that builds up on a rock or sculpted surface over time, either as a result of burial or because of exposure at the surface to weathering by water, wind, ice and salt. In the case of the Kouros, one would expect it to have developed a patina over the thousands of years it should have been buried. This is, of course, assuming that it is not cleaned or chipped off in some aggressive conservation treatment, something that was all too often done, particularly by early conservers, dealers or owners. For different rock types, what the mineralogical and chemical features of such corrosion layer are likely to be is to a great extent known and published. Of course, this again means that forgers also can access the necessary information to be able to recreate a convincing fake patina. Nevertheless, sometimes scientific analysis can reveal an artificial patina, when the wrong minerals or a modern binder or adhesive is used.

It is sometimes possible to get a chronological date from a patina. Absolute dating of patina would in effect show when it started to build up, and therefore when the carving was made, and provide a good clue to an object's authenticity. In ideal circumstances, isotopic dating can be used to give an age for the weathering layer on a rock surface. Cosmogenic nucleides are isotopes (for instance, of the elements beryllium or aluminium) that are produced in situ within a rock surface due to bombardment by cosmic rays. The concentration of these isotopes measured in the patina thus provides a direct measure of the time the sculpture has been exposed to cosmic rays at or near the surface. The restriction is, however, that an object must have been continuously exposed since fabrication to produce an accurate measure of time. It cannot have been shielded from radiation and must not have been exposed prior to sculpting. This is a major caveat in dating objects from archaeological excavation contexts that have been deeply buried and therefore at least partially shielded. Other isotopes used in dating are in elements such as carbon or lead and are unstable and decay fairly quickly. The reason such isotopes occur on Earth is that they are continuously being produced on the planet's surface or in its atmosphere, either by natural processes or by the activities of man, as in the nuclear industries. If such short-lived isotopes are trapped in the patina on a sculpture as part of the burial environment, through exposure to the elements or by an artificial process, this would possibly offer a means to date the burial, weathering or manipulation of the object. In this way, a youngest possible age for a stone object can be obtained: as these unstable isotopes are not replenished in the closed environment of the weathering crust, they can only decay and decrease in activity, until none are left.

All these methods, however, do not date the sculpture in absolute terms. A patina develops only post-sculpting, and can take some time to start appearing in any environment. The date calculated for a patina will hence always be younger than the final stroke of the chisel. What this technique can demonstrate effectively is whether a patina would be very young, say a few decades old. This would flag up serious issues with an object. Unfortunately, all absolute dating methods of sculpture patinas have yielded, at best, mixed results in terms of reliability and feasibility. Moreover, all these techniques require a sample to be taken and, while some systems show great promise, they still require too big a sample, several grammes in weight or about the size of a peanut. For the curator, the possibility of obtaining a date is not important enough to risk such severe damage to the object. Therefore, absolute dating techniques have to be ruled out for dating the patina on the Kouros, even though the resolution required is not high (it is either decades old or thousands of years). The available absolute techniques are either not applicable because the Kouros should have been buried or too experimental to warrant certain damage to the object. Instead, work has concentrated on characterising the patina and attempting to say whether such patina is consistent with an object of its age and suspected provenance.

Work on the patina from a "how would this form?" point of view has seemed to be more promising. As discussed above, analysis including of oxygen and carbon isotopes had determined that the stone of the kouros is dolomitic marble, and the provenance the island of Thasos at the Northern end of the Aegean Sea. This is a correct material for the time and region; it is "consistent with an ancient date". The Getty asked a distinguished marine geochemist, Stanley Margolis, from the University of California at Davis, to take some microsamples of the patina on the dolomite, to characterise them and propose how long they might have taken to form. Margolis noticed that while the bulk of the Kouros was dolomitic and therefore relatively rich in the element magnesium, the patina had very little magnesium in it – it was essentially calcium carbonate, or calcite. This surface effect can happen over time and is known as de-dolomitisation, where interaction with water in the soil leaches out the magnesium in the forming patina, to leave a calcitic crust. To Margolis, this could happen only over centuries or even millennia, therefore the patina was old and the Kouros very likely to be genuine. This was part of the evidence that convinced the Getty to buy the Kouros in the first place. However, work in the early 1990s showed that it was possible (if difficult) to produce this de-dolomitised patina in the laboratory, effectively meaning that the patina could be fake after all. Further work again suggested that other patinas might be present on the Kouros, a calcium oxalate crust that might (or might not) have been produced by acid washing the statue. All this just goes to show how difficult it is to determine the date of a stone object even, as is the case with the Getty Kouros, when money, means and time are not in short supply. This is not a fault of the scientists or the curators. They are all genuinely exploring the limit of scientific knowledge of how patinas form on stone in various conditions. All this work only shows that, beyond some general rules, we just do not know.

In an attempt to resolve the issues with the Kouros, Frel's successor as curator, Marion True, invited a group of thirty-one specialists from throughout the World to Athens to discuss the Kouros and voice an opinion. There was no consensus, but perhaps the balance of opinion, despite some loud and pointed comments to the contrary, was slightly in favour of the object being genuine. Those who were looking at the style of the piece were torn by the fact that it had features of multiple different kouroi ("Four Kouroi in one?") and there was much discussion of defects, deficiencies and incongruities. However, this was certainly far from a knockout blow. On the scientific side, Jerry Podany, a distinguished conservation scientist based at The Getty, stated that "most of what we observe on the kouros appears related to long-term alteration processes and to ancient surfaces", although he conceded that the surface was "odd when compared [...] to other kouroi". His laboratory made "over 200 attempts" at replicating the patina and all were apparently easily identifiable as fake under high magnification. A further paper pointed out "that despite the application of such a variety of technical examinations and analytical studies applied to the Getty kouros, not a single piece of evidence has turned up that would indicate that the surface alteration is of modern origin and has been produced by artificial patination", supporting Podany's view. The final scientific paper, however, concludes with a line which might be said by any scientific researcher in the field, "we need substantially more research before we can with confidence accept or reject a stone sculpture on the basis of technical evidence alone". As the Getty website reported, "Neither art historians nor scientists have been able to completely resolve the issue of the Getty Museum Kouros' authenticity".

This left the Kouros in a very odd position. It could not be proved that it is genuine, and it could not be proved that it is a late forgery. The story bounced back and forth and the Kouros remained in limbo, unable to be vindicated, but unable to be damned. In a peculiar way it resembled the cat in the imaginary thought experiment known as the Schroedinger's cat paradox. The paradox was created by the Nobel prize-winning physicist Erwin Schroedinger. It was a thought experiment to explain how strange the micro-scale, quantum world is. In his imagination, he placed a cat in a box with a vial of poison, with a Geiger counter and a radioactive substance. If the radioactive substance decayed it would be detected by the Geiger counter, which was wired to break the vial of poison, releasing it and killing the cat. In other words, if a single atom of a radioactive material decays, the cat dies. The death of the cat therefore depended on what happened on a subatomic, quantum scale. This was predicted by the Copenhagen Interpretation, which stated that the only way to know what was going on at that scale was to observe it. Before you observe, the atom is in both states and only when you look is it in one – the act of observation affects the experiment. Therefore, until you open the box, the cat must be in both states, both alive and dead, revealed to be either dead or alive only when you look. Schrodinger used this idea to show how difficult the relationship between the quantum world and the macro world is.

The Kouros was in an analogous position where it was both dead and alive, both fake and looted, and no-one appeared willing, or able, to look into the box and find out which was true. Its label in the Getty Museum (Getty Villa, Malibu, inv. no. 85.AA.40) reflected this, reading "Greek, about 530 B.C., or modern forgery". Interestingly, one might have argued that this was the only solution that would allow The Getty to keep it on display. If the Kouros was proved to be genuine, it was highly likely that it was looted, and one could be certain that the country of origin would put forward a highly emotive and politically damaging case that it should be returned. The Getty would be embroiled in another argument that would undoubtedly hit the press and arouse the ire of the American Institute for Archaeology (again). Alternatively, if it was proved to be wrong, a fake, then why would such a spectacular and wealthy museum as The Getty have it on display? The only explanation was effectively to state that it could be either – thus it stayed on display and was hugely appreciated by the many who saw it each year.

There are wider implications of the difficulties The Getty had got itself into. With all large collections, especially those bought mainly from the art market, one wonders how many of the ancient artefacts on display might have more complex and troubling histories than the simple date on the card next to the object. It is very likely, almost certain, that every museum contains objects that are not what the label says they are. Stone, when it does not originate from a known, documented, excavation context, is probably the most difficult material in which to distinguish in absolute terms the real thing from a copy or fake; see other chapters in this book where this "prince of materials" for forgers has been used. While the weathering layers and patina on a statue could be correct, or the stone used consistent with the period, their measurable mineralogical or chemical properties virtually never provide a watertight case for the authenticity of a sculpture.

As to those involved in the case, as mentioned above, Jiri Frel never returned to The Getty. He moved to Italy, but lived subsequently in Paris, Budapest and Rome. He lost touch with the academic world that he so much wanted to be part of with his clever, but illegal, scheme to create the Getty study collection and his aggressive acquisitions of high-value objects of questionable authenticity and/ or provenance. When he died, the first line of his obituary in the *New York Times* described him as "mercurial and eccentric". The *LA Times* mentions his involvement in acquiring "some of the museum's most problematic pieces – among them the Getty Kouros, a statue widely believed to be a fake... Frel kept a low profile since leaving the Getty". A final blow to his memory came in December 2018, when Italy's highest court ordered that The Getty should return Frel's favourite, the *Victorious Youth*, to Italy. As this book is being written, The Getty continues to assert its right to retain it, most vociferously in a press release from 3 December 2018, where it says, "we will continue to defend our legal right to the statue. The law and facts in this case do not warrant restitution to the Italian government [...] the statue is not and has never been part of Italy's cultural heritage. Accidental discovery by Italian citizens does not make the statue an Italian object".

Frel's successor, Marion True, attempted to revise the "optical due diligence policy", with more effort put into looking into the backgrounds to objects. She was, after all, one of the first to spot that the Kouros documentation was suspect. However, purchasing policy remained aggressive with the buying or receiving of countless objects, including some major, complete collections. One of the most interesting of these was the collection of Barbara and Lawrence Fleischman, an important collection of ancient Greek and Roman art, one of the best in America. This included around 300 objects and everything from statuettes to vases and jewellery in ceramic, stone and metal. The collection was exhibited by The Getty and published in a catalogue entitled "A Passion for Antiquities". The catalogue and the Getty website describe the collection as "among the most important in the world" and the Fleischmans as "Guardians of the Past". The first chapter, authored by True, discusses the Fleischmans and makes an awkward read to the modern, European eye. It is overwhelmingly adulatory and over the top, as "they collect on the basis of instantaneous emotional response to the object's aesthetic appeal...", translating to the fact that they buy what they like. It continues that "...such an approach demands great confidence and discernment, skills of connoisseurship acquired over decades of experience and exposure to works of art", and not just a lot of money and, as we will see, a particular attitude to provenance.

❝ Returns to The Getty over recent years have shown it to be changed hugely. The creation of the Getty Centre on a hill high above Brentwood with spectacular views over LA is the most major. Now there are new laboratories and galleries and space for the visitor to sit outside in the California sun. The Villa has also changed. Gone are a lot of the gardens, and in their place hundreds of tons of concrete and stone that make up new tourist facilities: restaurants, shop and lecture hall. Prominent among them is the Lawrence and Barbara Fleischman Theater, celebrating and memorialising two of The Getty's most important benefactors. Drawing loosely on a classical style, it is used to provide entertainment and education throughout the year.

However, all was not well in The Getty. The attitude towards aggressive purchasing was radically changing, with countries such as Italy and Greece clamouring to receive justice from looters and those who paid them. In 2005, Marion True and Robert Hecht of Euphronius Krater fame, were indicted by the Italian courts for conspiracy to traffic stolen antiquities. They were accused of importing into the USA dozens of objects that they knew to be looted from sites in Italy. The primary evidence for this came from a raid on a warehouse in Geneva that turned out to contain a fortune in looted antiquities and links to many museums and dealers. The owner, Giacomo Medici, was tried and sentenced to ten years in jail and a fine of 10 million Euros – the biggest fine ever in an antiquities case. In 2006, True resigned from The Getty and The Getty returned many significant pieces to Italy, including many pieces from the Fleischman collection. As the American Institute of Archaeologists had pointed out at least ten years earlier, "92 percent [of the pieces in the Fleischman Collection catalogue] have no archaeological provenience [provenance]", so there was no open knowledge of where they came from prior to their appearance on the market. Greece also filed charges against True and laid claims to Getty objects. Neither True nor Hecht ever went to trial – under the statute of limitations, the courts took too long bringing the prosecutions together. There were reports that True would reveal secrets in a biography. "Disgraced Getty Curator Marion True Roars Back With Tell-All Memoir" roared the *Observer* in December 2015. However, we can find no trace that the book has yet been produced.

As a final note, it must be emphasised that The Getty was not the only museum to get itself into trouble in this way. It might have been an extreme, but what it was doing was fairly common practice at the time. The Met, perhaps the "senior" museum in the USA, eventually returned the Euphronios Krater to Italy, where it went on display at the National Etruscan Museum and for the first time ever in Europe. Claims for many other objects are still going through courts in various countries. Suspicions that museum objects are in fact looted or are modern fakes are ongoing problems for all museums, particularly those whose collections are largely sourced from the art market. The Lawrence and Barbara Fleischman Theater still carries that name and the Kouros stands, only a few tens of metres away, admired by the public. Or it did until very recently. While this book was being written, The Getty withdrew the Kouros from display. The *New York Times* reported that the J. Paul Getty Museum Director, Timothy Potts, did not mince his words, "It's fake, so it's not helpful to show it along with authentic material", he said. Interestingly, unlike in the defence of the *Victorious Youth*, The Getty has issued no official press release about the Kouros. It has let it relatively quietly slip away.

Is this the end of the Kouros? Not necessarily, as we often see that successor curators and directors want to rehabilitate objects – making their name by showing that their predecessors were wrong. However, maybe not in this case because, as discussed above, if not fake then it is almost certainly looted. It is a shame, if understandable, that it is no longer on display, as it was a spectacular object with a very interesting story. Apparently, it can still be seen "on request".

Chapter 4
Turin Shroud

On Sunday, 21 June 2015, Pope Francis was in Turin, in northern Italy. He was paying a two-day visit to the city, where he would be praying at the tomb of the Blessed Pier Giorgio Frassati and celebrating the birth of Saint John Bosco. However, these were probably secondary to the main reason for the visit, and certainly secondary in the media's reporting of it. This was because the relatively new Pope was going to visit the Cathedral of Saint John the Baptist and pray before the famous Shroud of Turin. Before his arrival he donated funds for two busloads of "homeless and sick pilgrims" to visit and "prepare the way for the Pope's visit which is scheduled to take place on June 21: his poor arrive before him", an Italian newspaper, *La Stampa*, reported.

What the Pope saw in the Cathedral was a single sheet of ivory-coloured cloth, with indistinct brown markings. The cloth is nearly 4.5 metres long and just over a metre wide. When the Pope saw it, it was displayed in a glass-fronted, dark-coloured display case, wall-mounted and dramatically framed against a deep red, blood-coloured cloth. After kneeling before the object, he approached it and reached up to touch it, but was rather thwarted by the fact that it was mounted too high – with a stretch he managed to touch the frame. When Pope John Paul II saw the shroud in 1998, he said the mystery surrounding the cloth forces questions about faith and science and whether it really was Jesus' burial linen. He urged continuous study. Pope Benedict XVI described the cloth as an icon "written with the blood" of a crucified man.

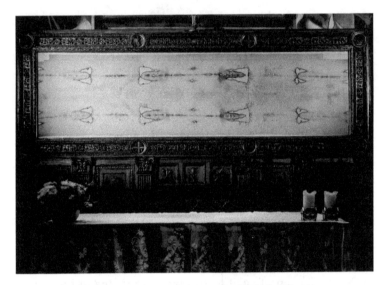

The Shroud on display in the Cathedral of Turin.
Picture by Paolo Gallo.

The fascinating thing about this object is that it is widely revered by many, who regard it as a genuine relic illustrating the suffering of Jesus Christ on the cross. However, to the majority of scientists, especially those who have even passingly studied it, this is clearly a medieval forgery. Some would go further to say that it was deliberately made for financial gain and to dupe pilgrims into paying their respects. In other words, it is an out and out fake. So what is this mysterious and highly contentious object?

> *In the interest of balance, I must confess early on connections with this, the most controversial of all the objects discussed here, which has sparked by far the most vituperative of debates. I was in Oxford as a student when the Shroud was being dated there, although I had nothing whatsoever to do with it, looking on from a great distance, lodged as I was in a completely different academic department at that time. However, I was to return*

to Oxford later and to end up in the Research Laboratory for Archaeology and the History of Art, then headed by Professor Mike Tite, who is central to the Shroud story. Mike was my doctoral supervisor, and I worked with him at RLAHA for ten years. I still see him regularly, although he has retired, and we still write papers together. Not only that, but for most of my time in RLAHA I shared an office with key members of the Oxford Radiocarbon Accelerator Unit (although I am not a radiocarbon specialist), and again this led to fascinating discussions, grant applications, books and papers. To some this will make me, and the account here, irretrievably biased. However, we are more interested in this volume in how people react to objects, real and fake, and how their lives have been shaped by contact with them, rather than proving the object right or wrong. We obviously have opinions, but the interesting point, especially with the Shroud, is why do people hold other opinions?

The Shroud – the undisputed facts (?)

As mentioned above, the Shroud is a long, rectangular piece of linen cloth with a characteristic "V" shaped weaving pattern, known as a herringbone twill. Although hard to make out immediately, it has on it the faint image of a naked, recumbent man, with his hands resting on his groin. It is a double image: half of the Shroud shows the front of the man, the other half his back. The man has shoulder-length hair, with a centre parting and a beard. He appears to be well built and is probably relatively tall; estimates have varied, but are usually around 180cm. The cloth also has reddish-brown stains which appear to be associated with the body – they look like bloodstains. These are particularly clear on the man's forehead, his hands and feet, and by his right side, but cover the body too. Another obvious feature of the cloth that Pope Francis saw is that there are a series of large holes in it, arranged in approximate pairs and relatively evenly spaced. These holes are the result of fire damage that occurred on 4 December 1532. The Shroud was housed in a silver reliquary in the sacristy when a fire broke out, and so severe was the fire that it partially melted the reliquary and this molten silver burned the cloth, resulting in a series of holes. These were patched by the local Poor Clare nuns, who added a backing cloth to reinforce it. These patches remained in place until removed during conservation work only in 2002.

Fortunately, these holes do not interact too much with the image. It is also obvious that there are repairs and/or damage to the edge of the cloth in places, and that the cloth is attached to a newer looking, whiter material.

This piece of cloth is obviously linked with the crucifixion and burial of Jesus Christ. The New Testament records that Jesus was scourged or whipped (Matthew 27.26 and others), he had a crown of thorns pushed onto his head (Matthew 27.29) and was then crucified (John 19:18). After he had died, his side was pierced by a spear to check that he was dead (John 19:34). All these wounds are dramatically and graphically depicted on the cloth.

The New Testament says something of the burial too. John says that Jesus' body was taken by Joseph of Arimathea and was wrapped "with spices, in strips of linen" (John 19:40) or, in other accounts, "in a clean linen cloth" (Matthew 27:59, similar to Mark 15:46 and Luke 23:53) and placed in a tomb from which he was subsequently resurrected. The Turin Shroud is clearly supposed to be the cloth mentioned in these passages. The only question to be asked is, is it? Or is it a relatively modern copy, made up to look like the "clean linen cloth" mentioned here?

History of the Shroud

The Shroud has a fascinating and well-established history, independently studied by two eminent medieval scholars, Canon Ulysse Chevalier and Herbert Thurston. Back to 1453 the Shroud's history is very clear. In that year it came into the possession of the Savoy family, an important ruling house that included King Umberto II, the last King of Italy. It was first obtained by Duke Louis I of Savoy and his wife, Anne de Lusignan, given to them by Margaret de Charny. When Louis died in 1465, his son inherited the Shroud and set it up in the Sainte Chapelle of one of the Savoy family castles at Chambery in France. The Chapelle was remodelled in its honour and gifts flooded in from visitors and pilgrims. Following the extension of the Savoy family's influence in the mid-sixteenth century, the new duke, Emmanuel Philibert, moved his capital from Chambery to Turin. The shroud soon followed, arriving on 14 September 1578. Its home has been the Cathedral in Turin ever since, apart from short visits elsewhere and a longer exile to the Abbey at Montvergine during the Second World War. No-one doubts that the Shroud Pope Francis venerated is the same object that Emmanuel Philibert brought to Turin in the fifteenth century; that is certain.

What is much less clear is where the Shroud was before 1453. It was certainly in existence before this date, and the work of the two aforementioned learned scholars has pieced some of this earliest history together. In 1453 Margaret de Charny was given a castle and some estates in return for some unknown service. It is widely thought that this "service" was the gift of the Shroud to the Savoy family. Margaret acquired the Shroud from her father, Geoffrey de Charny II, and grandfather, Geoffrey de Charny I. These are a fascinating pair. The contemporary author, Jean Froissart, in his hugely important *Chronicles* gave a vivid description of Geoffrey I. Amongst the knights of the French King, Geoffrey I was described as "the wisest and best knight of them all". He served as an emissary from King Jean II to the English enemy at the Siege of Calais in 1346-7, and then fought at the Battle of Poitiers on 19 September 1356. This was one of the most important battles of the whole medieval period and Geoffrey was at the heart of the action. Being specially favoured by the French King, he carried the King's personal battle standard. This was almost certainly the *Oriflamme*, a sacred standard of the medieval French Kings, which was designed to strike fear into the hearts of the enemy, as when it was raised tradition dictated that no prisoners could be taken – all would be put to the sword, noble or commoner. Thus, Geoffrey I had a key role next to the King at the battle and is depicted frequently in this role.

However, things did not go well. At the height of the battle the English men at arms charged the advancing French lines, causing chaos. The King and his son, Philip (then only 14), were caught in the charge and surrounded, along with Geoffrey I. Froissart described Geoffrey's end – "Fighting gallantly near the King... the whole hunt was upon him... The French were so overwhelmed by their enemies that in places there were five men at arms attacking a single knight. Sir Geoffrey de Charny was killed, with the banner of France in his hands". The King and his son were captured and were to spend many years as prisoners in England whilst the French negotiated a ransom for their release.

Geoffrey I was the first clearly identified owner of the Shroud. The reason we know this is down to another fascinating document, written in 1389 by Pierre d'Arcis, Bishop of Troyes. The de Charny family seat was at Lirey, twelve miles from Troyes and in the Bishop's diocese. The document discusses the activities of the canons of the collegiate church in Lirey, which was founded by Geoffrey I in 1352, four years before his death. In that church the canons were accused of displaying a cloth described as the likeness of the "sudarium" of Christ. A sudarium is a sweat cloth, but the canons were privately saying that it was the actual shroud of Christ, and this was attracting pilgrims and money. Investigating, the Bishop found that the canons had done this before, investigated thirty years or more ago by his predecessor, probably when Geoffrey I had still been alive, or, if not, soon after his death. Then the canons had been very direct, openly claiming to have the true Shroud of Christ. They had been the cause of an early investigation by Henry of Poitiers, D'Arcis' predecessor. D'Arcis concludes in his manuscript, "Eventually, after diligent enquiry, he [Henry of Poitiers] discovered the fraud and how the said cloth had been cunningly painted, the truth being attested by the artist who painted it, to wit, that it was a work of human skill and not miraculously wrought or bestowed". So Henry seems to have actually talked to the faker, and the De Charny Shroud was well known as a later copy. This line was supported by the circumstantial evidence that the de Charnys, while distinguished in valour, were far from rich, and they refused to reveal how they had got hold of such a fabulous object as the Shroud. If they had been able to tell a convincing story, that might have settled the matter in their favour. They either could not or would not. Either way, as far as we know, they did not. The fact that the canons withdrew the Shroud from display after Henry's initial intervention does suggest that they knew it was "not right". D'Arcis complained to Pope Clement VII about the Shroud being redisplayed. However, the de Charnys had sought permission from the Papal Legate (without going through D'Arcis, which must have rankled), and the Pope allowed the continuing display, so long as it was as only a likeness, not the real thing. So it was displayed.

The problem is that before Geoffrey I, in the early fourteenth century, there is very little further knowledge of where the Shroud came from. The complete story probably died on the battlefield of Poitiers with Geoffrey. Despite some very thorough investigation, there seem to be very few leads at all, but there are some imaginative ideas. Perhaps the best are those that link the Shroud to the Templars and/or the "Mandylion".

Any good story about knights in the Middle Ages, especially connected with the Crusades or the Holy Land, seems to feature the Templars at some point. The "Order of Solomon's Temple", or Knights Templar, were a military/religious order founded in 1120 in Jerusalem with the aim of defending the pilgrim routes to the city from attack. From a small beginning, the Templars became a large, elite, fighting force, hugely rich from pilgrim gifts and papal blessings. However, by the end of the thirteenth century the Templars were losing ground in the Levant to concerted attacks by the Mamluks, abandoning Jerusalem and then, by 1303, all bases in the Holy Land. However, they were still very much a political power, with "Houses" in most major Western countries and it is this that was to cause them considerable problems.

On Friday, 13 October 1307, the French King, Philippe VI, swooped on Templar houses in France and arrested all the Templars. They were accused of various things, including spitting on the cross, homosexuality and worshipping idols. Intriguingly, this allegedly included rituals involving the depiction of a bearded human head. Under torture some confessed, but it is interesting that many of the charges, and there were many, echo those used against other of Philippe's enemies. Two Templars are particularly interesting: the Grand Master (head of the Order) and the Preceptor of Normandy (head of the order in that Area, under the Grand Master). Under duress, they confessed to the charges, and in 1314, after serving over seven years in prison in Paris, they, with two other important Templars, were sentenced to life imprisonment in what looks like a show trial. On hearing their sentence, the Master and Preceptor recanted their confession. This made them lapsed heretics, which was punishable by death, and Philippe was happy to oblige. Without further petition he sentenced them and they were burned to death that same day, on the Ile des Juifs in Paris. They refused all offers of pardon and were so brave in their deaths that they were afterwards declared martyrs by some. The intriguing part of this is the name of the Preceptor – he was called Geoffroi de Charney, also sometimes spelt Geoffrey de Charny. This is obviously not Geoffrey I or II, neither is it Geoffrey's father, who has been identified and was called Jean. In fact, no clear familial link can be established, but the name is striking. Could the Shroud have been passed down by the Templars to Geoffrey I as a distant relative of an important Templar official? Could the Shroud be linked to the mysterious bearded head that the Templars were accused of heretically worshipping? Some think it is possible, and have written lengthy books about it. Certainly, the coincidence of the name is striking, but unfortunately no familial link can be established.

The Mandylion was another image of Christ on cloth, supposedly miraculously wrought. However, to most it was only the face of Christ. The story of how the mythical image came about is linked to Abgar, a legendary king of Edessa. He seems to have owned an image of the face of Christ, perhaps painted, perhaps miraculously wrought, which seems to have been present at Edessa in the sixth century CE and later. It appears later in Constantinople and is associated with the Crusades. However, it is also entwined with stories about St Veronica. According to extra-biblical tradition, St Veronica saw Jesus suffering on the long walk, the *Via Dolorosa*, to where he was crucified. She took her veil and wiped his face, imparting a miraculous image of his face onto her veil. In Church tradition, this is now commemorated in Station Six of the Fourteen Stations of the Cross, which were (and are) widely displayed in churches. The important part of the story here is that the Mandylion/Veronica stories do have a longer tradition of a physical object being associated with them. Ian Wilson, in his hugely enjoyable book, carefully winds the Shroud and the Mandylion/Veronica together, showing that if the Shroud was folded in a certain way only the head would be visible, so it might look like the Mandylion/Veronica. The object with early references might therefore be the Shroud, filling that annoying 1300 year gap where there is no reference to it. However, there is very little evidence for this link. The simpler story is without doubt that the Shroud has no established history before the fourteenth century CE, and after that a very clear history.

Chevalier and Thurston, the scholars who did such an exhaustive study of the Shroud's history, were "unwaveringly certain that the Shroud was a fourteenth century forgery".

85

Science and the Shroud

For such a high-profile and important object, it is amazing that it took so many years for anyone to be allowed to examine the cloth properly from a scientific point of view. The Turin authorities would not allow access. In 1969 this changed, when a "commission" of ten men and one woman were allowed close and lengthy access to recommend conservation and scientific approaches. They were chosen by the Cardinal of Turin, and they were all local – the Cardinal could have had almost any scientist in the world to do this, but he chose no-one based more than a few tens of miles from Turin. It was done secretly, the names of the commission not being released for seven years (although they were widely leaked). They described the cloth in detail and tried to determine whether there was blood present and how the image might have been formed, amongst other things. Four years later, pollen samples from the surface of the cloth were taken to try to determine where the cloth might have been made. Early results showed that there seemed to be some connection with the Levant, which was a good sign for the authenticity of the object. At the end of the 1970s and early 1980s more work was carried out by an American group, who formed the Shroud of Turin Research Project (STuRP). This group of volunteers used a largely borrowed set of equipment to address similar questions to the 1969 examination. They published their report in 1981 and stated that they believed that the image was that of a real, crucified man, but how that image was produced "remains, now as it was in the past, a mystery". However, not all of those involved in STuRP found the Shroud convincing. Walter McCrone for example, using simple microscopy at the onset of the investigations, found pigments such as iron oxide and vermilion on the Shroud, and called it an artist's inspired painting. Meeting with great resistance, feeling he was not being heard, he resigned from STuRP.

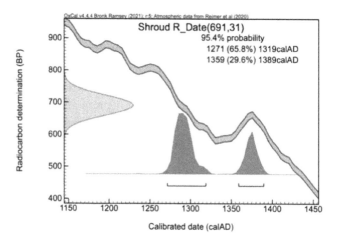

*Calibration of the Shroud's weighted average radiocarbon date,
showing the possible calendrical dates for the Shroud.
The dates are slightly different from those published.*
© Andrew Shortland & Patrick Degryse.

For most scientists, the key technique that had the potential to resolve this issue was radiocarbon dating. Radiocarbon was developed
in the 1940s and has the potential to date "anything that once lived".
It relies on a radioactive isotope of carbon, Carbon 14. Carbon 14
is very rare; in modern living things there is only around one atom
of Carbon 14 for every 1,000,000,000,000 atoms of the other two,
much more abundant, isotopes of carbon, Carbon 12 and Carbon
13. In life, Carbon 14 is present in all living things at a constant
ratio relative to the other two isotopes. However, when an organism
dies, it stops exchanging carbon with the atmosphere and, because
Carbon 14 is radioactive and spontaneously decays to Nitrogen 14,
its level, relative to the other isotopes, starts to decrease. After about
5730 years it will be half the amount it was in life – a period known
as the half-life of the isotope. Dating the Shroud should be a routine
task for radiocarbon dating, but it was not applied in the 1950s and
60s for one simple reason: sample size. The first technique used to
measure how much radiocarbon there was in the sample to be dated

was to "listen" and count the individual decays of the Carbon 14 isotope. For the Shroud, this would have required a large sample, the size of a large handkerchief or more – not an acceptable proposition. However, in the 1980s a new method of measuring was developed using a Particle Accelerator and a Mass Spectrometer. This "AMS" dating was much more efficient at counting and allowed sample sizes 100 or even 1000 times smaller than before – suddenly dating the Shroud seemed more possible, perhaps with a thumbnail-sized sample.

The STuRP group planned a series of studies to be performed on the Shroud, including carbon dating. They approached all laboratories with dating capacities, asking for their interest in the Shroud project. Six labs replied positively: Brookhaven, Harwell, Rochester, Oxford, Zurich and Arizona. In 1982, STuRP published a full list of tests to be performed on the Shroud, but quickly a disagreement arose between the group and the laboratories which would perform radiometric dating. STuRP wanted carbon dating only after another series of tests had been performed, while the labs involved saw the radiometric dating as the prime examination method, the only one suitable to give a definitive answer and making other tests superfluous. After all, why bother with other tests if everyone was agreed that radiocarbon dating could conclusively determine whether the Shroud dated from the time of Christ or not? At this stage, no-one in STuRP or the laboratories seemed to have any doubt that the technique would solve the problem.

In 1986, the so-called "Turin protocol" offered a compromise solution, indicating that carbon dating would indeed be the only test performed, and it would be carried out on the Shroud and control samples, which should be indistinguishable from each other. The test would be performed concurrently by seven laboratories, under the joint supervision of the Pontifical Academy of Science, the Archbishop of Turin and the British Museum. Proportional counting (the earlier technique, now with improved sample size) as well as AMS would be involved, on Shroud samples to be given to each laboratory, each weighing 28 mg (equivalent to 9 cm² of cloth), plus similar controls. The samples would be distributed by the British Museum. Laboratories would not communicate with each other during the analysis, or make any results known to the outside world until all results were compared and a joint announcement made.

In October 1987, however, the Vatican decided to adopt a different protocol altogether. Only two or three labs would be involved, using AMS only. The proportional counter method would not be used, as it would consume too much sample. In the end, the Protocol was a compromise between Turin's understandable desire to reduce the damage to the Shroud to a minimum, and the laboratories' desire to mitigate against errors and to be as certain as possible in the result. However, the discussions were strained at best and the laboratories cut out of the project were furious. Bad feeling, already bubbling under the surface, began to make itself felt. A letter signed by the laboratories clearly stated that the changes would only "enhance the scepticism of these critics" concerning the dating, but the Vatican insisted.

Dr Michael Tite from the British Museum had been chosen by the Vatican to act as an intermediary, to ensure that the samples were correctly taken and labelled and given to the laboratories. After much debate, on 17 April 1988 the journal *Nature* published the final protocol: the laboratories at Oxford, Zürich and Arizona would perform the test. The laboratories would have delivered to their representatives in Turin one sample weighing 40 mg, sampled from a single portion of weave. Sampling would be filmed. Each lab also received two control samples, but unfortunately they would be clearly distinguishable from the Shroud sample. In effect, the blind-test protocol could not be followed as the distinctive weave of the Shroud could not be found in any other materials in the British Museum or elsewhere. The laboratories would therefore know which was the Shroud as soon as they looked at the pieces of cloth. Disguising them by shredding the samples would create new problems, as subsequently treatment of the shredded samples to rid them of possible contamination could become problematic. In the end, did this really matter, as who would believe that knowing which sample was which could possible influence the laboratories in any way?

Perhaps the most significant difference between the final version of the analytical protocol and any previous ones was the decision to sample from only a single place on the Shroud. This means that, should the chosen portion be in any way not representative of the remainder of the cloth, the dating result would be applicable only to that portion of the Shroud, and have no meaning for the remainder... Harry Gove, director of the Rochester laboratory, not selected by the Vatican, argued in *Nature* that this change of protocol would expose any result – whatever it may be – to the suspicion of unreliability.

Samples were taken on 21 April 1988 in the Cathedral of Turin in the presence of Cardinal Ballestrero, four priests, archdiocese spokesperson Luigi Gonella, photographers, a camera operator, the laboratory representatives and Michael Tite. Giovanni Riggi cut the samples, while Franco Testore weighed them. A piece of 81 mm × 21 mm was cut from the Shroud, of which an outer strip showing coloured filaments of uncertain origin was discarded. The remaining cloth, weighing 300 mg, was divided into two equal parts. One half was preserved in a sealed container in the custody of the Vatican, in case of future need. The other half was cut into three equal segments and packaged for the labs in a separate room by Tite and the Archbishop. The laboratory representatives were not present at the packaging process, in accordance with the protocol. The three control samples were also supplied to the labs: a fragment of an Egyptian burial cloth previously carbon-dated to 1100 CE, a piece of mummy bandage dated to 200 CE and a fragment of the cloak of Louis IX of France, with a verifiable provenance and woven between 1240 and 1270 CE.

The Zürich, Arizona and Oxford laboratories performed their analyses respectively in June, May and August of 1988 and sent their results to the British Museum. On 28 September 1988 Michael Tite communicated the official results to the Diocese of Turin and the

Sancta Sedes in Rome. On 13 October of the same year Cardinal Ballestrero announced the official results in a press conference, dating the Shroud to 1260-1390 CE, with a 95% confidence level. The complete report was published in *Nature* in 1989 and called the results of the three laboratories mutually compatible. The combined age range of 1260–1390 CE coincided well with the known first certain display of the shroud, but obviously much later than the death of Jesus Christ.

Immediately many technical and other aspects of the dating procedure were challenged, the most obvious ones being the selection of the laboratories and the sampling process. Let's have a closer look at some of these objections…

The samples do not represent the whole

Suggestions have been made that the sample was taken from a medieval repair, perhaps in indistinguishable weave, rather than the original image-bearing cloth. Several scientific papers have been published since, suggesting that the sample may not have been representative of the whole, up to stating that what was analysed was "the worst possible sample for carbon dating". Conversely, when the Shroud was treated in 2002 Mechthild Flury-Lemberg, as head of the restoration and conservation project, rejected the theory of the "invisible reweaving", calling such repair technically impossible without leaving traces, and effectively finding no such traces in her study. The official report of the dating process states that the sample "came from a single site on the main body of the shroud away from any patches or charred areas". There were experts on hand when the sample was taken whose key role was to ensure that the sample was taken from the main part of the cloth. It is very unlikely that it was not.

The samples were swapped

Unfortunately, some "investigators" connected with the Shroud have decided that if they cannot attack the scientific arguments, they will attack the people – instead of playing the ball, they play the man. This will be discussed later, but the suggestion is that Mike Tite, and presumably the Archbishop too (it is never clear), swapped the Shroud samples for medieval ones. Let us leave aside for a moment the libellous nature of this suggestion and consider just the practicality. Some sleight of hand would have been needed but, more importantly, the highly distinctive cloth of the Shroud would have to be matched with a medieval equivalent – we know it could not, as discussed above.

The laboratories conspired to give a false result

It has been openly admitted that the analysis was not blind. As mentioned above, no cloth could be found that matched the highly distinctive weave of the Shroud. So the laboratories knew which sample was the Shroud as soon as they saw it. Not ideal, perhaps, but where is the harm? The only possible way it could affect the outcome is if you believed that all three laboratories conspired to suppress the "real" date and substitute a medieval one. This seems vanishingly unlikely and, as Harry Gove, who was involved both in the invention of radiocarbon dating as a technique and in the Shroud dating project, later stated, "lack of blindness in the measurements is a rather insubstantial reason for disbelieving the result".

The sample was contaminated

While the carbon dating technique in itself has not been challenged, what was dated in the experiment run on the Shroud samples has been. Suggestions of contamination by bacteria, organic residue, fire or even candle smoke, skewing the radiocarbon date towards the present, have been called in to explain a false date. However, the samples were carefully cleaned with strong chemicals before testing, and a simple mass balance will show that, even if contamination remained, about two thirds of the sample measured would need to be modern material to change the result from the first c. CE to a medieval date. Such gross contamination, in any form, would very likely be visible to the naked eye, let alone under the detailed microscopic investigation that the sample was subjected to. Harry E. Gove wrote in the journal *Radiocarbon* that "probably no sample for carbon dating has ever been subjected to such scrupulously careful examination and treatment, nor perhaps ever will again".

The statistics are wrong

Over decades, many hypotheses have been put forward to explain in a scientific way why the date could be skewed, but none of them have been shown to hold any ground whatsoever. Criticism, perhaps justly so, has also been aimed over several decades at the calibration of the measurement results and possible statistical errors in the final date or date range published in *Nature,* next to the accompanying relative significance level or reliability of the result. Amongst other studies, a paper published in 2019 by Casabianca and colleagues in the journal *Archaeometry* looks at the raw radiocarbon data used for the original *Nature* paper again. The data are stored at the British Museum, and repeating the statistics these authors indicate inconsistencies in them, not agreeing with the 95% confidence level claimed in the original paper. Most of the researchers looking at the statistics of the analysis do not make a claim that the Shroud is much older. They do, however, make a case for the fact that the results compared between the different laboratories are not as consistent as previously claimed, and that therefore a new analysis round to get (more) conclusive evidence is needed.

In the end, while many technical issues have been raised, and some have elements of validity, none of them can possibly make the carbon date obtained even two hundred, let alone more than a thousand, years older. We are, admittedly, refraining here from discussing at any length the many unchecked, unrepeated, unsubstantiated, unverifiable and irreproducible theories, experiments and new dating methods that have been hurled at the Shroud to prove any point. Nothing leads to the conclusion that the work published in 1989 was wrong, but it is apparently not perfect either – but would any scientific study be, faced with this level of scrutiny?

Radiocarbon as the prime technique

There are some other major causes of Shroud disputes. To most scientists, especially those who run radiocarbon laboratories, the radiocarbon date trumps all the other evidence put together. Scientists love quantification, and radiocarbon offers science a very precise way of explaining a date and a very clear percentage chance (given that the analysis is carried out correctly in all respects) of the object being right or wrong. To the laboratories the date is overwhelming evidence, and they cannot conceive of any circumstance where it could be contradicted, therefore other techniques are irrelevant – the job is done, the Shroud is medieval.

However, believers might take radiocarbon merely as one strand of evidence among many. Hence they might say, "but it is impossible that the image could be faked in the medieval period". To them, this "impossible" rates equally to the "impossibility" of the radiocarbon date being wrong – to the scientists it is not even close. Repeatedly radiocarbon scientists are asked, "well, if it is medieval, then how is the image formed?". Most attempt some sort of answer, and some get themselves into trouble because their answer is not a good one. However, what they are almost all thinking is, "I do not really have much idea, because I am only a radiocarbon scientist! Since it is definitely medieval, I am not really that interested in how the image was formed. I have moved onto many new projects now…". There is a fundamental disconnect concerning the importance of the radiocarbon evidence, and neither side really seems willing to understand the other's position.

Politics, language and personalities

Understanding is not helped by the use of language by both sides and problems with this can be traced right back to before the analysis was carried out. As outlined here, STuRP were central to early scientific work on the Shroud, and although a good deal of their work has not been formally published, much of it remains pivotal to arguments about the image, blood stains and pollen analysis and so on. They expected to be fundamentally involved in the dating of the Shroud in 1988, which was to be only part of a whole raft of other techniques that they wanted to apply. In the end, they did not have a chance. As discussed above, the radiocarbon scientists saw little value in the other techniques when radiocarbon would give a clear answer, and in the end the Church decided that the radiocarbon analysis alone would go ahead, effectively shutting STuRP out. This was not popular, and it left a very disgruntled set of scientists, many of whom were believers in the Shroud. Second, but perhaps less politically damaging, was the reduction of the number of laboratories taking part from seven to only three. This left out both proportional counter laboratories, but also the AMS laboratory at the University of Rochester in the USA. Harry Gove at Rochester had been fundamental in setting up the protocols and a main driver in getting the work done, yet he too was shut out of the final analysis. Perhaps the decision was not to use two American laboratories, so a choice had to be made between Rochester and Arizona.

Harry Gove recounts his bitter disappointment in his book, *Relic, Icon or Hoax? Carbon Dating the Turin Shroud,* but while critical of the detail of the work he is fair. In the end he concludes in another paper that radiocarbon dating "has achieved its greatest success to date in establishing that the Turin shroud is of medieval origin and certainly not the burial cloth of Jesus Christ".

However, perhaps the most serious error was that most of the academics in their laboratories and museums did not really appreciate the storm of media interest, good and bad, that would descend upon them following the dating. For many of them, while interesting, this was just another object to analyse and was treated as such. Very few realised that every word spoken, every action made, every gesture and nod, would still be analysed thirty years after the event. Nowadays, comments are posted for all to see on the internet, the veracity of the comment unchallenged and apparently unchallengeable.

CC We have spoken to a number of scientists involved in the dating, and the great majority are reluctant to get involved in a discussion about the Shroud. This is because they discovered long ago that whatever they say, the likelihood is that it will be used against them in the future. They have mostly therefore taken the option of not commenting further at all, and I have to say that I can sympathise with their position. I am sure that more than a few of them regret getting involved in this at all, simply because the project just will not go away. As far as they are concerned, the date is clear.

Most of the attacks have been made against Mike Tite, the British Museum's co-ordinator of the dating. The reason for this is that if you are going to attack the date, then tampering with the samples, however ridiculous that is, is the only approach really open to you. However, there is another character who was involved who certainly did not help the "healing" after the dating was carried out. This is Professor Teddy Hall, who was Director of the Oxford Laboratory at the time. Teddy Hall cropped up in the Piltdown Man investigation, where he used his new XRF technique to show that the fragments had been artificially stained. Indeed, it was the success of the Piltdown investigation that led directly to Teddy being encouraged to found the Oxford Laboratory in the first place, with the support of Lord Cherwell, Head of the famous Clarendon Laboratories. What Teddy learned from this was the importance of publicity in financing a laboratory.

Teddy Hall was a very interesting character whom I met only a couple of times relatively late in his life. He was an old Etonian of independent means and thought. He came from a wealthy family, whom he details in his privately published volume Some Memories. *He lived with the family at Shipton Court, the 1,000 acre Oxfordshire estate that his Mother "ran in a very Edwardian fashion" – the servants included "cook, undercook, two scullery maids, butler, footman, odd-man, housekeeper, a lady's maid and about six housemaids, a chauffeur, ten gardeners, and two rough gardeners". It all sounds very Downton Abbey. His father was a big game hunter turned war hero, leaving Sandhurst in time to fight at Mons in 1914 and fighting right through on the Western Front until 1918, uninjured but winning two Military Crosses and three Croix de Guerre. His brother (Teddy's closest companion and friend) died at Anzio in 1944 serving with the Irish Guards. Teddy had a lot to live up to.*

He was privately wealthy. To increase the staff in his Oxford Laboratory he simply gave up his salary and created another post this way. When he retired, he raised a million pounds to found a Chair at Oxford to make sure the Laboratory continued. He was famous for his parties at his house, where homemade fireworks on a spectacular scale were a common feature. He collected scientific instruments, Chinese porcelain and cigarette cards, flew hot air balloons and dabbled very successfully in constructing his own scientific equipment in specially built rooms in his house. He resembled the "natural philosopher" and gentleman of the eighteenth century much more than the post-war Oxford academic. But service on the Boards of the British Museum, the National Gallery and others made him politically astute.

The chance to date the Shroud must have struck Teddy as a similar opportunity to the experience he had had with Piltdown. He was certainly very keen to publicise the results and talk about them, perhaps more than any of the other scientists involved. Looking through the cuttings from major newspapers, one is struck by how many times Teddy Hall appears. He was certainly one to give a good quote for the newspapers and enjoyed twisting a few tails. His most famous remark about the Shroud was a possibly exasperated response to the same question that the scientists were (and still are) continually asked – how was it made. In a British Museum press conference he said, "There was a multi-million-pound business in making forgeries during the fourteenth century. Someone just got a bit of linen, faked it up and flogged it". While this is possibly true, it could have been more politically phrased. It was the sort of quote loved by newspapers, but was not going to help relationships between Shroud believers and sceptics. Teddy just loved the idea of using good science to "debunk" any idea that was not rational, "Some people may continue to fight for the authenticity of the Shroud, like the Flat Earth Society, but this settles it all as far as we are concerned", he said. Again, comparing Shroud believers to the Flat Earth Society is never going to help the arguments.

So where are we now? The Roman Catholic Church has always taken a rather sensible line on the Shroud, stating that it has value and is an inspiration for Christian believers whatever the date might be. There are still several active groups promoting the study of the Shroud, most of which are made up of believers in its authenticity. Many of the scientists involved are reluctant to make statements, fearing that they might be misconstrued. Speaking before the dating to *The Times*, Teddy Hall said, "If we get a medieval date then we shall know it is a forgery and we can relax and forget the whole business". However, this has not been the case for the scientists. Some have had hate mail, one senior scientist being accused of changing the date, "in your hatred you tried to fix the matter", "your whole credibility will be lost together with your job". There are many unfounded allegations on the internet. In 1996, Walter McCrone wrote that he had learned one lesson from studying the Shroud: never to make a similar study of any religious relic. He states that "the possibility [a relic] is real is slim, while belief in its reality does no harm, so let's leave relics to help those who need them". Perhaps this is the lesson of the Shroud.

For us, it is the only object in this book we have not seen ourselves. We did contact, through colleagues and friends in Theology and Canon Law, a number of academics and clergy in various Pontifical Institutes and academies. Though all answers we did receive were very polite, most declared themselves not experts in the matter, and referred to other colleagues (sometimes people we had previously written to). In this way, eventually, all lines went cold, and we gave up. As a good colleague wrote to us, "What an intriguing topic ... not only in times of alternative facts and fake news ... [but] The Vatican lays low when it comes to the authenticity of the Shroud".

Chapter 5
The Vinland Map

In the course of writing this book, we have met with many coincidences, almost as if the subject was chasing us, rather than the other way round. Too many coincidences, it sometimes feels, still to be random? It is the sort of reasoning associated with conspiracy theories or, in fact, fakes and forgeries. In this field, coincidence is rarely accepted for what it is.

Engaged on something of a lecture tour down the East Coast of the USA, unusually we were exploring the delights of the Amtrak rail system. Travelling by train from Boston to New Haven and then on to Baltimore, we were discussing the table of contents and title of this book. We couldn't yet agree on a suitable title, getting no further than a rather uninspired "Fakes and Forgeries", copied directly from the name of a postgraduate module we teach. Agreeing on the fact that this could only be a working title, we did agree on the cases we would describe in detail. One of them had to be the Vinland map, an alleged early fifteenth-century parchment map showing the contours of the known world and drawn from an unknown Norse source.

Making good use of public wireless internet on our train, we went about looking for the current location of the Map in question, only to find that it was on its last days of exhibition in the Mystic (Connecticut) Seaport Museum. From there it would return to the Beinecke Library of Rare Books and Manuscripts at Yale University, the very same academic institution we were on our way to visit. Our train, as we were browsing the web, literally passed within a few miles of the Map. How is that for serendipity?

A map based on Norse observations would be unusual enough as it stands, but what makes it unique is the fact that it includes part of east-coast North America, "*Vinlanda Insula*", and suggests that it was discovered by "*Bjarni and Leif in company*". Thus the Norsemen were the first Europeans to set foot in North America by hundreds of years. Based on cartographic and philological analysis, it was suggested to have been drawn around 1440, thus predating by half a century the discovery of the Americas by Christopher Columbus in 1492. The map even raises suspicion that he might have heard prior whispers of the continent from the mapmakers or their sources... Though it is now well-known that Norse explorers did effectively reach the New World, as evidence of their settlements has been discovered in Newfoundland (e.g. the site of L'Anse aux Meadows), this was not yet the case when the Vinland map first appeared on the art market in 1957. The artefact was destined to be controversial, at best.

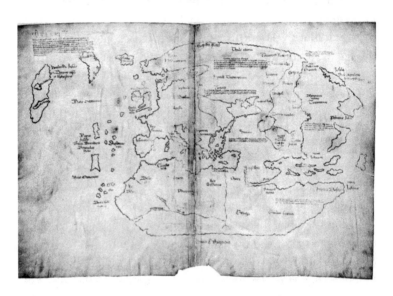

The Vinland Map, 27.8 by 41.0 centimeters.
Public domain.

When it first came to light, the map was bound together in a modern binding, likely dated to the nineteenth or twentieth century, with a medieval text called the *Hystoria Tartarorum*, or *The Tartar Relation*, an account of an expedition by Friar John de Plano Carpini to the Mongols in 1245-1247. The bound texts were unsuccessfully offered to the British Museum by London-based book dealer Irving Davis in the name of dealer Enzo Ferrajoli de Ry. Instead he went on to sell the volume for $3,500 to American collector and dealer Laurence Claiborne Witten II. As the positioning of wormholes in the map did not match the positions of those in the Tartar Relation, it was immediately treated with reasonable suspicion. The two texts had obviously not spent long together, likely less than 100 years. However, in the Spring of 1958, Yale librarian Thomas Marston acquired from Irving Davis a medieval copy of books 21 to 24 of the *Speculum Historiale*, the *Historical Mirror*, which had wormholes that precisely matched those of the Map. This showed that the Vinland Map had formerly been at the front of this volume and, what is more, the *Hystoria Tartarorum* had been at its end. The three documents therefore represented a sandwich – map, *Speculum Historiale,* and then *Hystoria Tartarorum* – and had been together for some considerable time before the centre section had been removed and the rest rebound. No traces of former ownership marks remained, except for an illegible part of a bright pink stamp overlapping the writing on sheet 223 of the *Speculum*. Witten, in turn, offered the Map for sale to Yale University, his *alma mater*, but would not reveal its provenance. Yale, unable to afford the asking price and concerned about the origin of the Map, contacted another (at the time undisclosed) alumnus, philanthropist Paul Mellon, to buy the Map (for a price later said to be around $300,000). He was to donate it to Yale University if it could be authenticated by the people who had seen the Map and books before: Raleigh Ashlin Skelton, Keeper of the British Museum's map collection, George Painter, a deputy curator of the British Museum who was first offered the Map, and Thomas Marston. Only Skelton had any expertise in the subject matter. Mellon insisted on absolute secrecy during these proceedings.

In this way, unfortunately, he effectively made any support from academic specialists in the evaluation of the documents impossible.

After years of study, the academic publication, *The Vinland Map and the Tartar Relation,* was ready. Mellon donated the Map to Yale, and on the day before Columbus Day in 1965 the Map was revealed to the world. Immediately, academic reviewers of the publications doubted the map's authenticity. In 1966, a Vinland Map Conference was held at the Smithsonian Institute, though the proceedings were not to be published until five years later. Concerns were raised about the actual content of the Map, depicting some well-known outlines of geographical areas (including Scandinavia) very crudely, while at the same time depicting uncharted territories in a most exact manner. Also, the Latin captions were more consistent with a seventeenth-century use of this language. Moreover, handwriting experts argued that the Map's captions and the writing in the *Speculum* and *Relation* texts disagreed, and suggested the handwriting style of the Map did not develop until the nineteenth century. Finally, at the conference it was also argued that it was unacceptable that since its discovery in 1957 no scientists had been allowed to study the Map and the accompanying texts.

It was not until January 1967 that scientists, from the British Museum, were allowed to investigate the Map and books, using non-destructive techniques only. Arthur Baynes-Cope, Principal Scientific Officer at the time, stressed in his report that scientific examination can only rarely produce positive proof of the authenticity of any object. Nevertheless, science may be able to say whether an object is consistent with its reputed origin, or whether it demonstrates certain inconsistencies or anachronisms in its structure or composition. Using low-power microscopes and photographic techniques such as ultra-violet and infra-red lighting, the British Museum Research Laboratory indicated that the parchment on which the Map was drawn had a "washed out" appearance, as if it were chemically treated. Subsequent testing, however, could not reveal any residue of, for instance, bleaching agents. Also, the wormholes in the parchment of the Map did not show the particular characteristics that can be seen in other ancient manuscripts, including the accompanying texts. It showed that the Map alone might have been treated with some agent. Moreover, the ink on the Map was described as having a 'peculiar structure', unlike the accompanying texts or any other manuscript of the period, showing indications of two ink components and an organic binder. The Map was not drawn with iron gall ink, typical of the area and period, or in any other substance known at that time. Black specks, as yet unidentified, were found but were considered to be particles related to outlining the Map, which would then have been inked over later with a yellow colour. Unless these could be proven to be metallic in nature, caused by using a lead, tin or silver pencil, these were suggestive of the use of anachronistic materials in making the Map. Finally, it was uncertain whether the two halves of parchment on which the Map was drawn, now held together with a binding strip glued to the back, had ever been a single sheet, which would be the case for any other known medieval double-page map. It was clear that no place names or features run across the fold, suggesting that the artist knew exactly where the fold would be.

By 1969, having had the opportunity to examine manuscripts written in all types of ink known, the British Museum scientists thought that the lines on the Vinland Map "did not have the properties characteristic of what was at the reputed date of origin of the map". The *Hystoria Tartarorum* and *Speculum Historiale* texts, conversely, showed no inconsistencies with the materials used at the time and in the area under investigation. The report concluded that it was highly probable that the leaf on which the Map was drawn was contemporary to the Tartar Relation, but had received treatment, drastic in nature, which no leaves of either book had suffered. The ink on the Map was unlike any other ink encountered in authentic medieval documents, and the presence of possible pencil marks underlying the ink could point to anachronistic materials being used. Research using more advanced techniques than those available to the British Museum Research Laboratory was suggested, focusing on the nature of the ink and the possible pencil outline, but in the meantime the report raised significant legitimate doubts about the authenticity of the Vinland Map.

In 1972, microsamples were taken from the Map and texts, to be analysed by McCrone Associates Inc. Dr. Walter C. McCrone founded this highly specialised microscopy consulting firm in 1956, considered to be one of the world's first analytical service laboratories. McCrone graduated as a chemist from Cornell University, and steered significant academic developments in the field of microscopy applied to chemistry. He is, however, best known for his forensic work and for analysing objects such as the Turin Shroud and the Vinland Map. The McCrone Group Inc. still exists today, dealing in mostly microscopy and materials analysis for industry and government. The company is still regularly involved in the authentication of archaeological objects.

For analysis of the Vinland Map McCrone Associates used the newly available microprobe technique. This X-ray fluorescence-based method bombards a sample with electrons, which causes the atoms in the material to give off radiation which is typical of its elemental composition. In this way it was shown that the ink in the *Hystoria Tartarorum* and *Speculum Historiale* texts is rich in iron and consistent with the use of iron gallotannate. The ink of the Vinland Map, however, is not iron-rich and is different from any other early ink tested. Moreover, the Map's ink showed a high content of titanium, quantified by McCrone Associates to range between 3 and 45 wt% in the spots analysed. Subsequently, X-ray diffraction analysis was performed on some samples. In this approach, X-rays of one wavelength are sent onto a sample, and are detected after they have diffracted on typical crystal structures in the material, thus identifying the nature of any minerals present. This showed the ink to contain the mineral anatase, rare in nature and white only when ground. Electron microscopy showed that the anatase was present as "smooth, rounded rhomb shapes identical in shape and size to the modern commercial pigment". Moreover, while natural anatase is usually associated with significant levels of iron and manganese, the type found on the Vinland Map was chemically pure. Electron microscopy also found the lines were drawn in two steps. First, a yellowish line strongly adhering to the parchment was applied, which was then apparently overlaid by a black line from which most of the pigment had flaked off. This countered the speculation of the British Museum laboratory, suggesting the black specks were the remains of a pencil guide line. The conclusion by McCrone Associates Inc. was simple: the inks on the Vinland Map contain substantial percentages of a pigment available in the observed form only since about 1920. While the parchment used may have been authentic, the design was not (though some thought was spared in the publication by McCrone & McCrone on the fact that the present map may be a copy of a similar original).

By 1987, discussions on the Vinland Map had truly escalated and controversy ensued. Cahill and co-workers published new PIXE analyses, stating that McCrone had been mistaken. This new, more powerful and more detailed chemical analysis technique, firing protons at the map to generate an X-ray spectrum typical of its chemical composition, suggested that the titanium contents in the ink were nowhere near as elevated as the original analysis had claimed them to be, but present only in trace amounts. Though the levels of titanium were slightly higher in the ink than the parchment, the occurrence of anatase would not have been the base for the yellow ink lines. The chemical composition of the inks used on the *Hystoria Tartarorum* and *Speculum Historiale* texts were, however, again found to be consistent with the use of iron gall ink, and are indeed different from the ink used on the Map. It was nevertheless argued that no anachronistic features were found, and that the previous suggestion that the Map was a forgery had to be re-evaluated. Stating that their work was by no means an attestation that the Map was authentic, Cahill and co-workers suggested that (again) additional scientific investigation could be performed, for instance by dating the parchment using the ^{14}C method.

The data of the McCrone versus the Cahill group were hard to reconcile. Both groups did make mistakes in choosing sampling locations and in their description of results (for instance, a member of the Cahill team did effectively find particles rich in titanium, but these were considered to be superficial contamination by modern material and were left unpublished). As the Cahill group were the first to apply PIXE as a newly invented technique for ink analysis, nobody at the time could explain the substantial discrepancy in the numbers. It is clear now, however, as PIXE data from laboratories around the world were gathered in the following decades, that the Cahill figures were wrong – all elements in the ink analysed were at least a thousand times too small. McCrone was right – the titanium values were very high, very likely too high.

In 1991 McCrone went back to Yale and took new microsamples from the Map to check his earlier results, and apply new techniques. He confirmed using detailed micrographs that the anatase particles were indeed a part of the yellow ink lines. Fourier transformed infrared spectroscopy was applied, a technique by which the infrared spectrum from a sample is recorded and mathematically processed, after which a component can be identified through comparison to a spectrum library. The organic binder in the ink was determined to be gelatine, probably of animal origin.

Having focused so much in previous research on the ink used in all the different documents, radiocarbon dating (see also the Turin Shroud chapter) of the parchment did not begin until February 1995. A strip of parchment weighing just under 29 mg was cut from the lower right corner of the map, far from any ink or marking. The sample was cut into several subsamples, which were chemically cleaned and processed for dating. As a test of the procedures, carbon dating of several parchments of known age was executed simultaneously to the work on the Vinland Map. This work took several years and eventually, in a 2002 publication, the parchment was stated to be CE 1434 ± 11 years, with a 95% confidence level of its age falling between CE 1411-1468. All dates obtained for the ancient "test" parchments proved to be in reasonable agreement with their independently known ages. Obviously, a fifteenth-century date for the parchment did not prove the authenticity of the Map, as this work dates the parchment and not the drawing on it, but at least the Map was still possibly correct.

However, remarkably, there are some points not usually reported about this radiocarbon dating. The first subsample used to date the Map was found to contain "bomb carbon", ^{14}C produced in the atmospheric testing of atomic bombs in the 1940s and 50s. Some part of the Map contained a material that was very modern. Chemical procedures were thereafter modified, and chemical cleaning intensified to be able to remove all this "contamination" and "properly date" the Map. This procedure was never disputed, but it took until 2017 for a sample of the Vinland Map remaining from the radiocarbon dating to be re-analysed, with the purpose of identifying the post-1950 contaminant. In the same study, the material composition of the parchment was further established. The very recent chemical contaminant was shown to be glycerol monostearate, a component likely coming from a hand lotion or from sun protection. The contamination thus probably originated from recent handling of the Vinland Map, possibly coinciding with its transfer from the market into the Yale library. In the same 2017 study, using an array of techniques, it was proven that the parchment was made from calfskin, and that its fibres are in fact in poor condition.

The scientifically measured fifteenth-century absolute date of the parchment coincided well with the presumed manufacturing of the map between CE 1431-1449, as suggested initially by Raleigh Skelton. As the very possibility of a technique such as carbon dating was unknown except to handful of specialists in the course of the 1950s, this match was considered to give extra weight to the believers' arguments. A forgery must have been made before 1957, when the Map came onto the art market. However, the dating of the drawing of the map to around 1440 was the result of seven years of scholarly work by Skelton, Marston and Painter. The forger could not have known that such date would be the outcome of this research process, and it could not be foreseen that a sheet of that date was to be used to draw the Map on. A coincidence in this matter was to some considered to be extremely unlikely and, in the eye of any believer, this was a clinching argument. Nevertheless, even the scientists who performed the carbon dating state in the reports and publications on their work that, although the date for the parchment is significant to the question of the authenticity of the Vinland Map, their dating research does not prove it. Nevertheless, one publication ends with the line that "declarations of the map's probable forgery should be seriously reevaluated".

In July 2002, soon after the publication of the carbon dating of the Map, a new analysis of the pigments used in the ink of the Map was published by Brown and Clark, work that had been performed almost simultaneously to the writing up of the dating research. Raman spectroscopy was used, a technique in which, by shining a laser beam onto an object, its interaction with the internal vibration of the molecules in the sample are measured. Different molecules vibrate differently under the same laser light, and this provides a structural fingerprint of the materials present in an object, to be identified by comparing them to a library of molecular vibrational frequencies. The analysis is entirely non-destructive, as the laser beam hardly penetrates the object.

Though the lines suffer from pigment loss, it was shown that the blank ink used to draw features on the Vinland Map consists of carbon, overlying a yellow line in which significant quantities of anatase are present. This material was not detected elsewhere on the Map. The Tartar Relation, on the other hand, is different and the ink used in this manuscript (probably) consists of iron gallotannate mixed with a small proportion of carbon. The rubrication in the book was identified as vermilion, a mercury-rich mineral pigment. Brown and Clark argued that before printing manuscripts were written in carbon-based ink or with iron gall inks. A common way of differentiating between the two is the fact that iron from iron gall ink can leach, causing discoloration and brown-yellow staining of a manuscript, making the paper or parchment brittle and fragile in the process, often causing considerable loss of substance. This is not the case with more stable carbon-based inks. If the Vinland Map had been drawn using medieval iron gall ink, one would expect the Map to show staining along the lines of writing, and some degradation. A clever forger would thus try to simulate the staining, explaining the two component drawing of the Map.

Confirming the presence of anatase only in the yellow ink lines, this mineral not being present elsewhere on the Map or even below the very surface of it (as the penetration depth of the laser beam is less than 0.001mm), was a blow to the authenticity of the Map, at the very same time the scientific dating of the parchment it was written on spoke in its favour. According to Brown and Clark, the presence of quantities of industrial anatase, a post-1920s product, in the yellow lines on the Vinland Map clearly indicated a twentieth-century origin. Various scientists have tried to explain how the anatase in the Map could be not a twentieth-century manufactured pigment but a natural product, but none of these theories seems satisfactory or credible.

In 2005, the Map was studied by a Danish team to recommend how it could best be conserved. This study made clear that the two halves of the Map were in fact made from separate sheets, though they later stated that "all the tests that we have done […] do not show any signs of forgery". This team, however, ignored previous studies rather than contradicting them. In 2004, Kirsten Seaver, reviewing all the available evidence to date in her book *Maps, Myths, and Men: The Story of the Vinland Map*, had already suggested that a forger could have found two separate blank leaves in the original *Speculum Historiale* (in which pages appeared to be missing), joining them together to form the Map.

    ❝ *To see the Map and the accompanying manuscripts with our own eyes, and to hear the story of their analysis first hand, we contacted our colleagues from Yale University and the Beinecke Library for a return visit. They immediately agreed to show us their objects. This time driving along empty stretches of New England road at 25 mph, we prepared for the interview.*

*Closely abiding by traffic rules, not to get stopped by the arche-
typical state trooper inevitably posted along these roads, we were
discussing why we were actually writing this book, and what to
expect once we arrived at New Haven. It led to the fundamental
question of what our book is in fact about. By the time we would
actually see the Vinland Map for ourselves, we would both already have a very good idea of the background of the Map and
the manuscripts, all of the many scientific techniques involved in
analysing them, and the standpoint of the different stakeholders.
Nevertheless, to effectively see, feel, smell... an object is always
an entirely different matter altogether. Each time you see such an
artefact, it leaves an impression that can be had only once. After
that first look, you interrogate the object, look at details, possibly
think of ways to approach the scientific question to answer. One
can look at an object again and again, for hours and days. But
you never again feel (or ever lose) that first impression it left. The
object speaks to you, it draws you in. That is what these objects
do, and that is what we as scientists love. And exactly that is
what this, our book, is about. How do people interact with these
objects? How do they change people's lives? We decided to ask our
friends at Yale not only to see the Map and manuscripts, but also
to inquire about the communications around them. Not only the
academic correspondence on the acquisition and testing of the
Map, but also the inevitable letters from the wider public. How
are people emotionally committed, and why? How do John and
Jane Doe feel about the Map, apparently in such a strong way as
to want to write to an Ivy League institution?*

The first impression of the Vinland Map, once you get to see it,
is one of an underwhelming nature. Our colleagues from the
Beinecke tell us this is almost uniformly the case. The Map is small,
unclear, and rather monotone. Apparently, at the Mystic exhibit,
many people asked where the Map was, standing right in front
of its display. It is rather unspectacular, while the accompanying
manuscripts are far more attractive to the inquisitive eye. Yet, people

interact with such objects like the Map in the most extraordinary ways. Misunderstanding the abbreviation UV of ultraviolet light for "ultraviolence", people wrote into the Beinecke to make pleas for it not being applied to this unique object. Boxes and boxes of letters from the wider public are kept at the Beinecke. There is more than enough material to warrent an investigation on its own. Some come from people occasionally writing in with impressions or remarks. Others come from regular writers, believers or not, on how to proceed with the investigation of such a marvellous object, or not. Strong characters and little old ladies alike are impressed with or appalled by the Map, and what it stands for. This is mostly harmless.

On a less comical and even downright harmful note, the Vinland Map was also the cause of great controversy and even hostility between the Scandinavian and Italian communities in the United States. Should the Map be real, it was obviously proof that the Norse people were the first Europeans to arrive in this part of the world (which they in fact were, as we now know from archaeological excavations in Nova Scotia). Conversely, Americans of Italians descent, claiming Christopher Columbus' discovery of the New World in 1492 as their own, saw a clear and obvious attack on their community in the US. The Map would then be a deliberate creation for this sake. Critical commentary was also aimed at Yale academics in their ivory towers. Secrecy and different versions of how the Map was offered for sale, escalating to outright lies by Yale alumni around the story of the Map, fuelled controversy. The fact that the sale of the Map to Yale and the initial investigation into its authenticity were performed on the basis of one's honour and "a handshake" did not shed positive light on academia.

Much correspondence is available on the initial acquisition of the Map. These include comments on its authenticity or its possible modified nature from the very onset of the possible sale. Some letters already in the 1950s suggest that the Map is not what it claims to be, and that Laurence Witten must have known this. Witten, on the other hand, even if he was convinced of the Map's authenticity (and thus its unique – i.e. expensive – nature), makes every effort to put up a smoke screen on its origin, and makes thorough scientific investigation difficult, to say the least.

In 2013, two pre-1957 references to the *Hystoria Tartarorum* and *Speculum Historiale* texts were reported and consequently published (in 2018) by Scottish researcher John Paul Floyd, giving clues to the origins of the books. Both texts are thought to be mentioned in an 1892-3 catalogue of a Spanish exhibition commemorating the discovery of the Americas by Columbus, on loan for the exhibit from the Archdiocese of Zaragoza. They are mentioned again in the posthumously published notes of Spanish priest Pérez-Pastor in 1926. Neither document mentions the existence of a map. When McCrone in 1974 declared the Map to be a forgery, the original bookdealer, Laurence Witten II, was asked by Yale to disclose its provenance and to discuss the possible return of Paul Mellon's money (which, in fact, Mellon never asked for). Witten could only refer them back to Ferrajoli de Ry, and stated he had no knowledge of any previous provenance. Ferrajoli could not provide further information: he was convicted shortly after the sale of the Vinland Map of the theft of ancient manuscripts from the Cathedral Library of La Seo, Zaragoza, and died shortly after his release from prison in 1967.

Discussion on the authenticity of the Vinland Map has raged on. The analytical data accumulated over years of scientific investigation show clear anachronistic features in the ink used to draw the Map. The Mystic exhibit was set up, describing the Map as a twentieth-century object. These arguments are countered and explained in rebuttals, in which more and more ingenious hypotheses, ranging from contamination by wild conservators to paint flakes falling from the storage ceiling, play their role. It seems to us that the very unlikely, if not the impossible, has been put forward to defend the Map's authenticity. But when all that is impossible has been eliminated, what remains, however improbable, must be the truth.

For a final touch of synchronicity: while we were finalising this chapter, an obituary of Professor Robin Clark appeared in the British newspaper, *The Times*, speaking of the "renowned inorganic chemist who pioneered a dating technique (actually not a dating technique but Raman spectroscopy, *red.*) that authenticated a Vermeer and exposed an ancient map as a forgery". While Clark's research was key to Raman spectroscopy becoming a regular part of the toolbox used to examine works of art, the authenticity of the Vinland Map is still not a settled debate. It is very likely that as many believers as disbelievers hold firm to their positions, as is usually the case with such objects. At the Vinland Map Symposium, the event coupled to the Mystic exhibition of the Map in 2018, Yale conservation scientist Richard Hark did confirm again that the ink lines of the Map contain varying amounts of anatase, calling this "consistent with modern manufacture". Moreover, anatase has now also been found on two small patches of the first page of the Tartar Relation, where the original iron gall ink seems to have been erased and replaced. Other academics at Yale have labelled the Map outright "unfortunately" a fake. As for a future place for the Vinland Map and its sister manuscripts, the Beinecke sponsors further research and display. It feels it has a responsibility to the artefacts, be they right or wrong. The Map will remain in the collection, to inform future researchers and to be available with all its analytical data to many (research) communities. As for a possible return to Zaragoza, this is not at hand at the moment. The Zaragoza library has effectively been decimated, and there is no longer a collection to go back to, though this is still looked into. Nevertheless, most authorities at Yale University refrain from commenting on the authenticity of the document. They continue to regard themselves as custodians of an extremely interesting and controversial document.

Chapter 6
The "Amarna Princess"

On 23 January 2010, a major London museum opened a rather unusual temporary exhibition. In it was a very striking object – a normal garden shed. Occupying most of the corner of one of the two rooms of the display, the shed was small, six feet by eight feet, sat on a small patch of fake grass and was "protected" from the visiting public by a twee wooden fence just about knee high. Looking through the open door of the shed, or one of the two windows, the public could see its remarkably clean environment. On one of the benches inside were paints, brushes and odd pieces of stone; on another finished and unfinished white stone statutes; and on a third some rather learned-looking tomes. From the statues and books, an Egyptian theme could be discerned – exhibition and museum catalogues with lots of big colour pictures.

The exhibition was called *The Metropolitan Police Service's Investigation of Fakes and Forgeries* and it was the result of a unique collaboration between the Metropolitan Police Art and Antiques Unit (MPAAU) and the host institution, the Victoria and Albert Museum in Kensington.

❝ The MPAAU is a small specialist unit based near Charing Cross in London. It consists of only a handful of officers who, through their dedicated work, look into crimes involving illicit antiquities smuggling, theft from museums and fakes and forgeries. Due to their small size, they rely on the help of academics in general and museum specialists in particular to do their work,

and work particularly closely with the British Museum, which takes the lead in studying and combatting the trade in stolen and looted antiquities. I have been involved in several cases with the MPAAU, but their work is sometimes constrained simply by their lack of resources.

In the Exhibition the shed was a centrepiece of the display as it related to one of the most prolific and talented forgers of recent times, Shaun Greenhalgh. When the exhibition opened, Greenhalgh was "serving time at Her Majesty's pleasure", although he was released soon afterwards. The shed in the V and A was a replica (not a fake or forgery), a copy of the one that Shaun had used in his crimes in the garden of his council house in Bolton in Northern England. It remains famous amongst a certain community. If you go online to Shedblog (subtitled "We love sheds!") and bypass the invitation to enter the Shed of the Year competition (by clicking "No thanks!"), then a picture of a slightly quizzical man in a suit sitting in the copy of Shaun's shed can be found, with the remains of Shaun's forgery process sitting around him.

The Egyptian books and the stone give a hint to the topic of this chapter, which begins thousands of years earlier and thousands of miles south of the wet and windy town that was, and is, Shaun's home. In 1351BC, the Egyptian King Amenhotep III died sometime in his forties or early fifties. He had reigned for 38 years, succeeding his father, Tuthmose IV (or Tuthmosis – there are several equally valid ways of transliterating Egyptian names), and had established Egypt as a great world power. This was perhaps the height of Egypt's influence. It would perhaps never again have such reach and political strength. Over this period of the Egyptian 18th Dynasty, father had succeeded son and the names had oscillated: Tuthmose III succeeded by Amenhotep II, succeeded by Tuthmose IV, succeeded by Amenhotep III. Sure enough, Amenhotep III had a son intended for the throne, another Tuthmose. However, Tuthmose died young and another son, also called Amenhotep, became the crown prince – the next king. It is possible that Amenhotep III and the future

Amenhotep IV reigned together as coregents for a period of years – Egyptologists debate this. But in 1351 BCE Amenhotep III died, perhaps after a series of illnesses. Certainly, neighbouring kings had been concerned for his health and one of the most powerful, Tushratta, father of one of his principal wives, had sent a magical healing statue of the goddess Ishtar to him to try unsuccessfully to help. The new King set about the traditional building programme of an Egyptian King, with temples at Karnak at the southern capital, Thebes (near modern Luxor), being constructed. Egypt had a polytheistic religion, with a complex hierarchy of gods and goddesses which throughout its history were more or less worshipped. During the 18th Dynasty of chief importance was the god Amen-Re; indeed the massive Karnak Temple is largely devoted to his worship. Amenhotep himself is named after the God – his name means "Amen is content". However, from early on Amenhotep IV seems to have had a fascination with another god, the Aten, represented by the Sun's disc. The Aten had been worshipped as a minor god for hundreds of years, and had become much more popular during the reign of Amenhotep's father, who has been called "the Sun King". Possibly Amenhotep IV was involved in this worship as a youth, probably as a priest. Nothing in this was terribly unusual, but what happened next was.

It is recorded on a rock stela on a hot and lonely cliff in Middle Egypt, miles away from the urban delights of the traditional capitals of Thebes and Memphis. It tells that in the fifth year of his reign Amenhotep IV instigated radical reforms, something never before or since seen in Egyptian history. He decided that instead of the panoply of gods that Egypt was used to, there should be only one – the Aten – and that he should be the High Priest and sole focus of the cult for all of Egypt. At a stroke, he reduced the power of the huge temples devoted to other gods and the extensive, influential priesthoods that supported and maintained them. Not only that, but he built an entirely new capital city on the banks of the Nile in this deserted spot half way between Memphis and Thebes. He moved the Royal Court and all its staff and constructed massive new temples for the Aten in radical designs. What the Court thought of this is not recorded; certainly it would have been unwise to record any criticism of such an absolute monarch as the Egyptian King. However, the equivalent of moving London, Washington or Paris to a desert backwater days from the bustle and civilisation of the centuries-old existing capitals could not have been popular. To this day the reason for him doing this is hotly debated, as is much else about his reign. Is this the action of some religious fanatic, a starry-eyed dreamer obsessed with a cult that he became involved with in his youth, or that of an astute politician, anxious to wrestle power from unwieldy and problematic religious élites and consolidate his own? Both have been argued and every shade between those extremes. Whatever the reason, the capital certainly moved, the religion was changed and the suppression of the worship of other, traditional, Egyptian gods began. Most significant perhaps of all, Amenhotep IV changed his names. He did away with all reference to the old god, Amen-Re, and changed his name to "Akhenaten", which translates as "the servant of the Aten". His new city he called "Akhetaten", or "The Horizon of the Aten". The remains of the city can still clearly be seen in the desert beside the Nile in Middle Egypt, close to the modern village of Amarna, sometimes called Tell el-Amarna. The short period during which the Egyptian capital was at this uninspiring spot is hence known to modern Egyptologists as "the Amarna Period".

There was another aspect of the changes that Akhenaten brought about that is central to our story. Not only did he change the religious life of his country, Akhenaten dramatically changed the way in which he, as King, and the Royal Family as a whole were depicted in art, both in statues and reliefs. We are all familiar with the way most Egyptian Kings chose to be seen. They are almost always depicted in the flower of youth, with splendid physiques and gently smiling, almost otherworldly, expressions. While there are minor exceptions, this is typical right through from the earliest depictions of Kings in the Old Kingdom to the last in the Ptolemaic Period nearly three thousand years later. There is one major departure from this well established norm, and this is the Amarna Period, and Akhenaten is responsible for it. To start with, the King himself is not depicted as the perfect human specimen. He is shown in a very stylised fashion, with very heavy hips and breasts, extended stomach and long, thin legs and arms. His head is shown elongated, with pronounced chin and top of the head. The whole Royal Family is so depicted, but not only that, they are shown in new ways too. Instead of the highly formal, religious scenes of earlier (and later) kings, Akhenaten is shown playing with his children (all girls, or at least only children depicted as girls are ever shown), and in discussion with them as they climb on him and his wife Nefertiti. The reason for these depictions is as hotly debated as the reason for the change in religion and they may (or may not) be linked. The androgynous depictions of the King (from statue fragments it is sometimes difficult to tell the King and Queen apart) and the fact that all the children shown are daughters have led to speculation about his sexuality. Could he have had a disease that was slowly changing his physique? Or was this simply the way he wished to be seen, but if so why? There are few answers and much academic and pseudo-academic speculation. What is clear is that the depictions of the Royal Family in this period are very distinctive, easily distinguished from those in other periods and other cultures. Since, as discussed later, this Period was relatively short, Amarna pieces are rare and highly sought after by collectors and museums. New finds on the open market are rarer still…

The Bolton Story

All this takes us back to Bolton, a few miles from where Shaun Greenhalgh's real shed sat. Bolton is a typical industrial town of Northern England. Of no great size or importance through most of its history, it is the arrival of the Industrial Revolution in the eighteenth century and the inventions of local boys Arkwright and Crompton that propelled Bolton away from being just a small market town selling wool. In less than a hundred years, it was a wealthy centre at the heart of the spinning industry, producing high-value textiles using the very latest technological advancements housed in some of the earliest factories. New communication links by canal and railway made sure that these valuable commodities could be easily moved to the coast, and hence by ship throughout the expanding British Empire and the wider world. All this brought money into Bolton and made some of its citizens rich men. As was traditional in this period, some of that new money was spent gentrifying the town. Earlier shacks and wooden houses were pulled down, and fine, stone townhouses in beautiful crescents that attempt to echo Georgian Bath and London were constructed. At the centre of this, as it had to be for most *nouveau riche* Northern towns, there needed to be something civic and something educational, something *improving*. Hence the building of a massive Town Hall, completed in the second half of the nineteenth century and added to and extended through the early twentieth to create "Bolton Civic Centre". Part of this on Le Mans Crescent is the Bolton Museum and Art Gallery, with its severe neo-classical, gently curving frontage. The Museum really started in 1876, when Samuel Taylor Chadwick, a local doctor, left the remarkable sum of £5,000 specifically to create a Natural History Museum. He was a noted philanthropist, having previously given generously to create extensions to the hospital and an orphanage in Bolton. The first curator was appointed in 1883, and the "Chadwick Museum" opened in 1884. Quickly the Museum expanded beyond natural history to take in anthropology, archaeology and especially Egyptology. The Museum still has an internationally important collection of ancient textiles, reflecting the source of the wealth of the town and the interests of donors and patrons. The Chadwick Museum was quickly too small, and with various moves and transitions, the main collections found their way to the new building in Le Mans Crescent in 1947. The Museum now holds over 400,000 accessioned objects, including an interesting Egyptian collection. It is at the Museum in Le Mans Crescent that a curious meeting took place that was to have severe repercussions for both parties.

In January 2002, a frail old man walked into the Museum for a meeting with the Keeper of Egyptology. In his 80s, George Greenhalgh drew a stone statue from the bag he was carrying and placed it on the desk. The statue was 51cm high and was of creamy-white stone. It was essentially the torso of a standing woman or girl, missing the head, all of the right arm, most of the left, and the legs and feet from the shins down. The proportions were odd, with very heavy hips, buttocks and thighs, light waist and curiously small shoulders and breasts compared to the rest of the figure. On the back, the figure seems to be resting on a short post, which has two circular drill holes in it, as though it was attached to something else at some time. At first glance the figure appears naked, but it is in fact clothed in a light, pleated, sheath dress that clings to the body as if it were elasticated. The right shoulder is bare and the bottom of a wig can be seen resting on it. Rather indistinctly, flat tassels can be seen showing how the dress was secured, and these run down the body and the post behind the figure. The Keeper identified the figure immediately as having all the characteristics of an Amarna period piece, a depiction of one of Akhenaten's daughters. There are similar statues of Amarna women in Philadelphia and especially the Louvre in Paris. The Louvre example is particularly similar, with the same missing parts, but in a red quartzite stone rather than the creamy white of Mr Greenhalgh's statue. Mr Greenhalgh revealed that the statue had been in the family for over a century, having been bought by his great-grandfather at a country house sale at Silverton Park in Devon. In 1892, the 4th Earl of Egremont sold off the contents of the house, which was then demolished in 1902. Mr Greenhalgh still had the sale catalogue for the house, which listed lot 201 as "eight Egyptian figures". However he said he did not know what the statue was and had been offered a few pounds for it by a dealer who wanted it for a garden ornament. The Museum showed the statue to a series of experts and then, with help from the National Art Collections Fund, the Friends of Bolton Museum and especially the government-funded National Heritage Memorial Fund, acquired it through the auction house Christie's in September 2003 for £439,767.

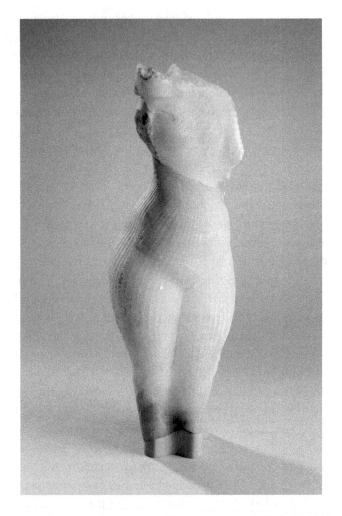

Amarna Princess, in imitation of figurines dating to 1350-70 BCE.
Bolton Museum.
Reproduced by permission of Bolton Council.

Called the "Amarna Princess", the statue had a short, starring role in an exhibition in London for the National Art Collections Fund, and then returned to Bolton, where it was displayed with due fanfare in the Egyptian collection.

The Princess declared a fake

❝ *In 2005, the Bolton Keeper retired, to be replaced by Tom Hardwick, and in 2006 I received a telephone call from him concerning the statue. Tom and I had met in classes at the University of Oxford, where we had suffered the indignities of trying to learn the Middle Egyptian language together – many, many classes trying to learn to identify and translate hieroglyphs. Tom had gone on to specialise in the study of Egyptian statuary, and I in Egyptian materials – glass, ceramic and stone. Tom swore me to secrecy, but stated that he had some suspicions about the statue. As a relatively new employee of the Museum, he was in a particularly delicate situation; this was their prized possession, recently acquired with much fanfare and expense – could it be "wrong"?*

From Tom's point of view, there were all sorts of things problematic with the detail of how the figure was portrayed. As a favour to an old friend, and because my interest was thoroughly engaged, I went up to Bolton to have a closer look. On my arrival, Tom took me into a small room and we examined the statue together with whispered voices. He talked me through his concerns. The statue's tassels were tied into a knot, which was poorly executed. This detail was important to Egyptian sculptors as the tassels secured the dress together – here it was casually treated. There were further problems with the way the tassels curved across the body and, most damning, the way the tassels continued across onto the pillar behind the statue. This showed a misunderstanding of what the pillar represents. The technical term is "negative space" – the pillar is not part of the figure at all and the definition between figure and negative space is always kept distinct. Bits of clothing never cross over into this space, which is used for independent inscriptions. Whoever carved the statue was not familiar with this vital difference, which was so central to the way Egyptian sculptors regarded the way their stat-ues "worked". Not only that, but while the tassels were confident-ly, if slightly unusually, depicted across the figure, on the negative space they were very sketchy. It is almost as though the sculptor had realised that he did not know how they should be depicted here, so his confident style left him.

From my point of view looking at the stone, the Amarna Princess also had problems. The pale, creamy stone used so commonly in Egypt is somewhat loosely termed "alabaster". It is familiar to anyone who has gone as a tourist to Egypt as it is widely available and still used to produce tourist souven-irs, whether these are vessels, ash trays or small statues. Many geological terms are somewhat inaccurately appropriated by archaeologists, and unfortunately most of them, because they have been used for so long, are hard, if not impossible, to eradi-cate. Alabaster is one such term, because it is applied in differing areas to what geologists would regard as two completely differ-ent materials. Most alabaster of the ancient world, that of Rome and Greece, is gypsum, a mineral consisting of calcium sulphate. However, the "alabaster" of Egypt is different. While appearing superficially similar, Egyptian alabaster is calcium carbonate, known as calcite. The Amarna Princess was made of a relative-ly uniform stone that did not have the appearance of the often banded and inhomogeneous Egyptian alabaster. Not only that but it was quite soft – calcite has a hardness of 3 on Mohs' scale, gypsum only 2. A fingernail typically has a hardness of 2.5, so it will scratch gypsum but not calcite. A small application of a fingernail to an unobtrusive part of the Amarna Princess showed that it was soft, more consistent with gypsum or a more friable calcite, less so with compact Egyptian alabaster. What is more, the surface of the stone was too smooth on the breaks – they had been artificially aged. In contrast, the drill holes, suppos-edly drilled in antiquity to mount the piece (in a very untyp-ical way), still had stone dust from the drilling in them. From both a style and a material point of view, the Amarna Princess *looked "wrong" – it was almost certainly not a genuine ancient Egyptian object. Tom later wrote an important academic paper on the Amarna Princess and the police involvement, from which a lot of this story is drawn.*

Meanwhile, behind the scenes, the Metropolitan Police Art and Antiques Unit, who would work with the V and A to produce the Exhibition, were becoming increasingly concerned about the activities of the Greenhalgh family. For some players in the art trade, the Greenhalghs had become all too good at finding what was supposed to be a lost antique or archaeological piece. When one dealer did not want it, they simply took it to the next – they were getting a reputation. Some thought it was highly likely that they, or some of their contacts, were making at least some of the pieces. However, the art world is naturally secretive and, either by accident or by design, this information was not available to all parties. The whole affair came to a head when George Greenhalgh attempted to sell three Assyrian reliefs to the British Museum. At first glance these appeared to be missing scenes depicting soldiers and horses from the Palace of Sennacherib at Nineveh. Initially fascinated by the objects, experts at the British Museum quickly uncovered some serious problems. The script on the reliefs was cuneiform, a particularly difficult script to fake easily, and there was a spelling mistake on the relief that no scribe would have made. Additionally, the horses were depicted with alarmingly modern-looking harness. The British Museum called in the police.

In March 2006 the Amarna Princess was quietly removed from display in the Bolton Museum, and very shortly thereafter the Greenhalghs' house was raided by the police. They found a wealth of incriminating material and pieced together a case against the family. Amongst this material was further alabaster figurines in the Amarna style: a headless torso of a princess holding an offering table, a further princess with a very unsuccessful attempt at a head, and the bust of a princess with side lock wig. In addition, there were sketches of Amarna heads and figures and paperwork concerning the acquisition of stone, including alabaster. It became clear that the family had been making, or at least passing on, suspicious material for at least 17 years before their arrest. So voluminous was their output that the term "Greenhalghiana" has been developed to describe it. It covers multiple periods, styles, materials and sizes. To quote from Tom's paper that studied especially the Egyptian material in depth:

> "In addition to the Egyptian objects [... other...] material included Romano-British and later metalwork; sculptures by Paul Gauguin, Barbara Hepworth, Constantin Brancusi, and the nineteenth century American sculptor Horatio Greenough; and paintings by the Scottish Colourist Samuel Peploc, Picasso, and the Lancastrian artist L.S. Lowry."

Amongst the most important pieces evidently made by the son, Shaun, and afterwards offered for sale by other members of the family, especially George, was the Risley Park Lanx. This was a supposedly Roman, rectangular, silver tray with a relief decoration. Described by an antiquarian in 1736, it was republished in a learned journal in 1981. The piece itself had been lost in the meantime, but was brought into the British Museum by the Greenhalghs, who stated that it had been in their family's possession since the eighteenth century. The British Museum bought it from them, against some high-profile detractors. One of these, intriguingly, was Teddy Hall (mentioned previously as a player in the Piltdown Man and Turin Shroud sagas). In his privately published memoir, the last academic memory Teddy puts down on the penultimate page is "the Risley Park Lanx". Since he was a trustee of the British Museum, Teddy had been asked his opinion on the Lanx. He recounts the story of its finding and states, "I immediately smelt a rat and said it was a deliberate fake". However, analysis at the British Museum showed that the silver it was made from was of a composition typical of Roman silver. Teddy, being Teddy, was also "Chairman of the Antique Plate Committee of the Goldsmiths Company", one of the twelve great Livery Companies of the City of London, and arranged for their experts to look at it. They found a series of problems with solder, corrosion and composition that Teddy highlights. He also pointed out the "curious coincidence that this object appeared a few years after a very comprehensive article had been published in [*The Antiquaries Journal*] about the lost Risley Park Lanx". Teddy's last sentence states, "to this day I am still convinced that this was an elaborate hoax". He was writing in 1999, and it is now widely agreed that he was right – it turned out that Shaun had made it, in his shed, from melting down ancient silver coins. The British Museum were of course not the only ones fooled; many museums, collectors and auction houses were taken in by the skill of the production and the plausibility of the "sales pitch". Who could doubt George Greenhalgh, such a nice, delicate, 80-odd-year-old man? And the British Museum were in good company, Greenhalghiana finding its way into the collections of the Institute of Art in Chicago and the Tate in London and fooling experts on both sides of the Atlantic.

In the police raid on the house the true extent of the forgeries was revealed. There was a furnace for melting metal or firing ceramics, modelling clay, fragments of stone and glass, and full colour reference books for Egyptian, Assyrian, Old Master and other art. However, as mentioned above, there were also further Egyptian figurines similar to the Amarna Princess. Two were found in the house itself: a standing princess figure, this time with a head and 63cm tall, and a 27cm high bust of a princess wearing a sidelock. Both appeared to be in a very similar stone to that of the Amarna Princess, but were less successful in their attempts at imitating antiquity. A final bust, this time in sandstone stained purple in an attempt to imitate red quartzite, was found gathering dust in the garden shed. This would have fooled no-one and was obviously a failure. Finally there was a photograph of a further attempt at an Amarna-period piece – this time a relief showing Akhenaten as a sphinx worshipping the Aten with inscribed hieroglyphic text. Again it is unconvincing, the layout and the inscriptions in particular later being described by Tom as "shoddy". However, the piece itself is missing, perhaps sold to a minor antiques dealer or passed off in a flea market or junk shop, where the Greenhalghs confessed to disposing of many of their pieces.

The search led to the arrest, charging and prosecution of the family and all pleaded guilty to the charges. Shaun confessed to making the objects and was sentenced to four years and eight months for conspiracy to defraud. George's role was as the "front man", the innocent face to draw in the mark – he was given a suspended sentence of twelve months. His wife, Shaun's mother, Olive, was given the same sentence, and another son, George Greenhalgh Jr., a suspended sentence of nine months for acquiring property with the proceeds of crime. The extent of the Greenhalghiana forgeries is still unclear. Some 44 objects were presented at the trial, but something over a hundred are known to have been offered to various buyers. The true number is probably significantly larger and will almost certainly never be known. Similarly, the amount of money made by the family is also unknown, estimates suggesting £1.0-1.5 million. Only around a fraction of this was recovered by the courts. However, the Greenhalghs lived a far from glamorous life – there were no expensive holidays (Olive claimed never to have left Bolton), no fast cars or expensive jewellery. The family lived together in a small council house. It is unclear how much of the rest of the money was actually recovered, or indeed how much there was originally.

Shaun, author and TV star

However, the story does not really end there. Shaun in particular became something of a celebrity, the "uneducated", amateur artist who fooled the art establishment, the experts of major museums and prestigious, Mayfair auction houses. How such a man could accomplish this was the topic of television programmes such as *The Antiques Rogue Show* and *Fake or Fortune*. He went on to write his own autobiography, *A Forger's Tale: Confessions of the Bolton Forger*, which for such a long book actually reveals very little about his technique, inspiration or motivation. It does back up, however, some of the conclusions of the police on how the Amarna Princess came about. When the police raided Shaun's house, they found a range of academic books and museum and gallery exhibition catalogues. Shaun is obviously still bitter and resentful at the police raid, although he says himself that "co-operation was, for the time being, out of the question", so he was not inclined to be helpful. He describes their search in detail, with one searching detective described as "like a monkey sorting nuts", finds treated with "a squeal of delight". Amongst the finds was a catalogue for a major exhibition at the Museum of Fine Art at Boston MA entitled *Pharaohs of the Sun: Akhenaten, Nefertiti and Tutankhamen* which was published in 1999. Object number 49 in the catalogue, depicted on Figure 8 is a beautiful image of the torso of a Princess. In the autobiography Shaun says that the Amarna Princess was made "in my Dad's garden shed the winter of 1999, a few weeks before the millennium… My inspiration for her was a beautiful red granite version in the Louvre". The Louvre piece (Louvre E25409) is a little smaller and described as "torso of a princess". Looking at them now, they are very similar. You feel that the near identical damage to the two pieces should have been suspicious. Both have the left arm preserved. but without the hand, no right arm at all and no feet. The differences are that Shaun's Princess is broken lower on the legs, so has knees, which are competently done, but also has the broken remains of the bottom part of a wig on the right shoulder. It does not take long to find the inspiration for these changes, because catalogues number 50 in the same volume is another princess sculpture, this time from the University of Pennsylvania (E 14349). Although less voluptuous than the Louvre piece, and in a style that is a less extreme version of Amarna art, the Penn piece has a similar diaphanous dress. Most importantly, it is broken below the knee, so giving a good idea as to what knees should look like. It also preserves the bottom of a wig on the right shoulder. Shaun's Princess is an amalgam of the two pieces from this book. Interestingly, they are both shown one above the other in the catalogue proper, on page 218. Shaun did not even have to turn the page to generate his chimera. The Louvre Princess is depicted not only in *Pharaohs of the Sun*, but also in another book Shaun had, *The Royal Women of Amarna*, where it is depicted twice, again frontally, but more importantly for the faker from the proper right side, a new view that reveals the depth of the figure. Shaun therefore had several images to work from as inspiration. It should be noted that the Louvre figure is in red quartzite, not granite as Shaun says in his autobiography, perhaps stone identification was not Shaun's strong point.

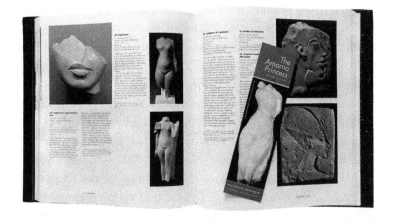

Pages 218-9 from Pharaohs of the Sun, *showing the two real figures almost certainly used as models for the Amarna Princess. Lying on the book is a bookmark, one of several different marketing media published by Bolton Museum to advertise the statue when they first received it.*

Source: Pharaohs of the Sun: Akhenaten, Nefertiti, Tutankhamen, Rita E. Freed and Yvonne J. Markowitz (1999), Museum of Fine Arts, Boston.

The autobiography also contained some very interesting but unsubstantiated claims. The most famous of these concerns *La Bella Principessa*, thought to be a portrait of Bianca Sforza by Leonardo da Vinci, but Shaun claims he made it basing it on a checkout girl in a supermarket in Bolton. See the chapter on the *Salvador Mundi* for more on *La Bella Principessa*. Following on from his "fame" in the programmes, Shaun realised that there might be a market for legitimate copies and his own original art. On 28 November 2017, the *Bolton* News, always a fan of the Greenhalgh story which it has repeated at length on many occasions, reported that Shaun was successful in selling his own works in an article entitled "Art lovers snap up legitimate works by Bolton master forger". Apparently, there was "keen bidding amongst fans of the talented artist's work" and the auction house manager described the auction room as "full" and "buzzing". We are told that "These days he is using his amazing talent legitimately, with his art works, clearly identified as being by him, sought after by collectors from the UK and abroad". Four works in what was described as "Lowry-style paintings" were sold and "netted him a total of £15,800". Shaun has painted such things before, and yet again the *Bolton News* is there with the story which was part of the arrest and trial reporting. The work was called *The Meeting House*, and the family created a false provenance for it, claiming that it was given to Olive on her 21st birthday by "her gallery owner father". Other letters forged by the family suggested that Lowry was a close family friend. The fake Lowry was spotted and sold for only hundreds or low thousands of pounds, but eventually unwittingly "changed hands for £70,000 when another owner claimed it was an original". Shaun continues to sell, or attempt to sell, his own works. He tried his own original work in 2018 and was supposed to be selling more in 2019, again in Bolton. We will see if the Bolton public remains as interested in his "talent".

❝I last saw the Amarna Princess "in the flesh" with Tom in that small room in the Bolton Museum. I occasionally talk to student classes about it, but it has obviously faded from my mind. It was therefore a great surprise when a number of years later I happened to be in the store of the Metropolitan Police Art and Antiques Unit, looking at other items for them. The store is in East London and is very secure with the type of security guard who impresses with their politeness, competence and obvious knowledge of what they are doing. The store is small and filled

with objects that are, or have been, the subject of police cases. It very much resembles the store of a major London auction house, with so many objects so close together it is often difficult to see what is there or what to look at first. As I turned around, there on the shelf at eye height was a plain, cardboard box with the words "Amarna Princess" on it in blue marker pen. Somewhat taken aback, I asked the officers whether that was THE Amarna Princess. "Oh, yes", I was told and they kindly took it down for me and opened the box. There it was, carefully wrapped in protective padding, safely stored. The Police were anxious to return it, and had been for years, but it was up to the lawyers to work out who owned it and in what circumstances it might be returned. This can be a problem for pieces and for the police. Who actually owns the statue, when so much public money has been spent from numerous sources for something that is "wrong"? If the money is all returned, who owns the piece then? Surely it does not go back to the forgers? Anyway, somehow this riddle was eventually sorted out, and I was very pleased to hear that shortly after this was successfully concluded, the Amarna Princess was returned to the Bolton Museum.

Ever keen to get the last drop out of a good story, the *Bolton News* covered its return when, in July 2019, the "Master Forger Shaun Greenhalgh … returned to Bolton Museum to say sorry". The "audacious" story is repeated again with "seasoned experts" fooled, although somehow the Princess is now the granddaughter of Tutankhamen rather than a sister or half-sister. Shaun "has issued an apology" and went back to the Museum with a television crew making a new BBC series. "Everyone has been very nice", he said. Coincidentally, the visit corresponded with the reopening of the display the previous year, after a £3.8m refurbishment. He was filming a new series with Waldemar Januszczak entitled "Handmade in Bolton" with ZCZ Films. According to their website, Shaun is set the task of forging increasingly difficult objects over four episodes from eagle brooches to rock crystal bottles.

❝ Obviously, I had to try to look up the television series that Shaun had made. It turns out that this series of four programmes was the latest in three series: "Handmade: By Royal Appointment" in 2016, followed by "Handmade in the Pacific" (2018), then "Hand made in Bolton", which shows you can always go one better. The four half-hour programmes covered ceramics, metalwork and stonework. I am never keen on these sorts of programmes; there are too many "Fakes in the Attic" shows and they vary from mildly sensationalist to just simply wrong. It is with a heavy heart that I therefore sat down to watch a couple of the episodes (I could not face watching all four). I was most interested in Shaun, but the rest of the "cast" rather got in the way at times. The narration by Januszczak himself fortunately fades largely away after the first few minutes. Unfortunately, Shaun has to put up with his co-presenter, an "Oxford historian". Her links to the University were stressed throughout, with shots of her walking past Oxford colleges wearing a gown. She is obviously working very hard on the presenting, and comes across, as a reviewer put it, "as though she is on speed". Shaun, on the other hand, comes across as knowledgeable and likeable, when he has a chance to get a word in edgeways. The shots of him on his own, talking to camera and explaining the techniques he is using, are by far the best. He comes across as considered and sensible, and is obviously skilled at what he does. His house is shown, and he still lives in a small "two up, two down" red-brick terrace house, presumably in Bolton. Again, the shots of him at home showed him as likeable and easy going. I was particularly interested to see the episode where he makes a copy of an English medieval alabaster carving from English alabaster, a gypsum-based stone from the Nottingham area, amongst others. He is shown going to the Victoria and Albert Museum to look through the cabinets for a piece to copy. Entirely co-incidentally, Vernon Rapley, who was one of the hated officers involved in the search of Shaun's house and rose to be head of the MPAAU, then moved to the V and A after retiring from the police. He is now

Director of Cultural Heritage Protection and Security there. It is tempting to wonder what their conversation might be if they met in the tearoom of the V and A. Somehow, I do not imagine that it happened. Whilst standing looking at the cases, the Oxford historian asks him, "Have you ever worked with alabaster?". There is a short, but pregnant, pause before Sean replies, "Er, yes, mainly calcite alabaster, the stuff used in Egypt". He then goes on to give an account of different alabaster types. Overall the alabaster programme is entertaining, especially when Shaun is on his own. Particularly fun is the string of expletives used when he accidentally breaks the piece several times. It makes this feel more real and closer to the work he would have done when he was still making things in order to defraud collectors and museums of large sums of money.

The Amarna Princess on display in the Bolton Galleries.
© Andrew Shortland & Patrick Degryse.

I wanted a final look at the Amarna Princess, so went back to the Bolton Museum, where it was kindly taken off display for me. It was much as I remembered it, but the question for the day was, is it calcite or gypsum? Shaun has made much about how he knows the difference between the two, and the Bolton Museum had heard that Shaun was claiming that the statue was "real alabaster", in addition to his laborious explanation about gypsum and calcite in the TV programme. This is a very simple analysis to be carried out, entirely non-destructively, by Handheld X-ray Fluorescence. The analysis showed in seconds that the stone of the statue contained significant calcium and sulphur, meaning that the Amarna Princess is indeed gypsum and not calcite, as was always suspected and published. The Princess was put back on display, where it remains a part of the museum collection very popular with visitors. Interestingly, it is displayed not in the main Egyptian gallery, but in a special area for fakes and forgeries, which seems a very good place to put this very interesting object.

So the Amarna Princess story has a happy ending, with the figure back in the place where it is most likely to be appreciated and admired, starring in a story that is nearly as good (if completely different from) as the one it would have had if it had really been made on that dusty desert plain by the Nile, three and a half thousand years ago.

Unfortunately, the story of Akhenaten and his family has a less than happy ending. Akhenaten died young, perhaps in year 16 of his reign, and without him things start to unravel fast. The city of Akhetaten was rapidly abandoned, the Court moving back to the old capitals. His son and heir, the young Tutankh*aten*, changed his name to Tutankh*amen*, and reinstated the pantheon of old gods – "normal service is resumed" in the priesthoods and temples. However, Tutankhamen also dies young, to be buried in a minor tomb in the Valley of the Kings. His successors start systematically to expunge the names of the Aten and anyone connected to the Aten heresy from the historic records. In a way that was completely mirrored in George Orwell's *Nineteen Eighty-Four*, the Amarna-period kings become "unpersons", their names are removed from king lists and later Egyptian historians missed them out completely, as though they never existed. Ironically, this whitewashing of the historical record may have had a significant role in keeping that insignificant little tomb of the "Boy King" Tutankhamen relatively safe. It therefore existed almost complete when, on 26 November 1922 Egyptologist Howard Carter shone his torch into the tomb to reveal the "wonderful things" within and start a craze for Egyptomania that is with us almost a hundred years later.

> *" A final footnote strikes me, a small but interesting point that does not seem to have been picked up in any of the texts written about the Amarna Princess. I believe I saw the Princess as it was originally mounted. Certainly the mount was subsequently changed to flatten the base and correct the slight tilt to one side that made the statue look a little odd. Thus the mount I saw, depicted in Figures 1-4 of Tom's academic paper, shows the three small drill holes towards the bottom at the back which are drilled into part of the negative space discussed above. However, these are unused and not how the figure is fixed to its wooden base. Instead two metal rods are used, one of which sensibly fits into an obviously modern hole in the broken base of the statue. This is an entirely reasonable place to put a fixing and there would be room for one or two more if the modern mounter, almost certainly Shaun Greenhalgh, had felt the need for a stronger fixing. However, that is not where the second fixing is placed. The second rod rises vertically from the base, behind the first fixing, and works its way straight up to enter a hole that is drilled exactly where the anus of the Princess would be. The rod therefore penetrates the figure between its buttocks in a way that might be regarded as "remarkable", and highly unusual. It is still mounted in this way. This is entirely unnecessary – there*

are many ways that are as good or better for fixing the figure to the base. It is almost as though a message, conscious or unconscious, is being sent. It is tempting to see that message as aimed at the art establishment, to all those experts who have accepted the Greenhalghiana, but denied Shaun his rightful place in art history. Perhaps the final laugh is Shaun's?

Chapter 7

Leonardo and the Eye

Salvator Mundi, Leonardo Da Vinci.
Picture by Jozef Klopacka.

On 15 November 2017 the auction house Christies ran an evening sale entitled "Post-War & Contemporary Art" in its saleroom in New York's Rockerfeller Center. It was in some ways a relatively small sale with fewer than 50 lots, but the sale rocked the art world and set a new standard for prices and for controversy. The saleroom was packed, every seat and standing space taken, even in the special overflow areas where the auction could be watched by live video feed. The sale started relatively quietly, but the sale prices reached were good: over $32 million for a Rothko, $11 million for a Bourgeois bronze. The eighth lot, a graphite on paper entitled *Lead Sea 2*, and tenth lot, "vinyl paint on vinyl tarpaulin with metal grommets", *Untitled*, both sold for exactly the same amount, $4,212,500 including premium. However, it was the lot between these two, Lot 9B, that everyone was there to see. Described as "oil on panel" and "25 7/8 x 18 in. (65.7 x 45.7 cm.)" in size, it was a depiction of Jesus Christ, shown from just above the waist up – a "half figure" to use the old-fashioned term. Christ raises his right hand in blessing and cupped in his left is a crystal globe. The painting has a classical title – *Salvator Mundi* – the saviour of the world, for the globe Christ holds symbolises the World. He is wearing a blue gown and cloak edged in gold embroidery, has long hair to the shoulders and stares directly into the eyes of the viewer. Even to the amateur the depiction is odd. The blessing hand seems beautifully painted, sharp and clear, and yet the other hand is blurred. The folds of the gown are again strangely variable in the way they are painted. The long hair is lustrous and sharp on his left shoulder, but the right seems much more casual. Above all what strikes you is the face. It seems to protrude from the darkness of the background, blurred and indistinct with eyes that are both hypnotic and difficult to define. What is also obvious to even the amateur is that this is not "post-war and contemporary art". If it is a genuine piece, the style and materials place it at 4-500 years earlier – it is an "old master". A hint as to why this painting is being sold in this auction is perhaps given in the estimate for the piece, a staggering $100,000,000. This sort of sum requires buyers that can pay this price, and they are more often found in modern and contemporary art than in old master paintings. The painting is here because this is where it will find an audience that can pay that sort of figure. The saleroom is packed because they all want to be there to see it sold. This is the height of auction house theatre, the reason some people love salerooms, and the hype has been carefully stoked up by Christies over the previous months with the painting doing a world tour, being shown to 27,000 people in San Francisco, Tokyo and London before coming to New York.

In charge of proceedings, like a concert conductor, is Jussi Pylkkanen, the auctioneer. Having warmed up the proceedings with works worth "only" millions to tens of millions, this is now the main event. Often to bid in sales you have to show that you have the money to fulfil your promise to buy before you are given a paddle with a number on it, which you will need to raise in order to bid. Highly unusually, Christies issued special red paddles to the elite few who were considered to be wealthy enough to bid on the *Salvator*. Equally unusually, this single lot was the subject of a special, 174-page catalogue extolling its virtues and comparing it to a whole range of other works of art and even, depicted on page 38, the Turin Shroud, which has a similar long-haired, frontal view of Christ. Pylkkanen started by introducing the painting as "previously in the collection of three kings of England, King Charles I, King Charles II and King James II", and what followed was pure theatre. Starting at $75 million, within twenty seconds Pylkkanen signals that it has passed the reserve price by saying "$90 million and selling" with $100 million shortly afterwards. Pylkkanen, leaning forward so far that he looks like he might topple off the rostrum, works the audience, taking bids from his colleagues on the telephones alternately on his far left and right, with stares at the main central audience in between. Bidding slows and he hints that "$150 million might have it", then "$160 million might have it". There are five bidders in, and then a call of "$200 million", which has gasps and cries from the audience. Pylkkanen has to hush them with a shush, a "please" and a raised hand. After this, the process slows down, with bids only every 20 seconds or so, sometimes longer.

The bidding seems to be down to two telephone bidders with the pauses filled by Pylkkanen's humour and irrelevant facts. From $260 million the bidding starts to go up by only $2 million a bid and is very slow. Then, suddenly, comes a leap from $270 to $280 million, then from $286 million to $300 million to cries and clapping from the crowd. "Let's see if that's done it!", says Pylkkanen. A long pause follows, almost 100 seconds which feel a lot longer, an interminable wait at an auction, and then the price creeps up again – $302, $310, $312, $315 million, as it crawls on. One bidder tends to bid in $2 million jumps, the other more impatient with larger jumps of $10 million or more. The last bid from this bidder goes from $370 to $400 million, an enormous jump when bidding had been mostly in $2-5 million increments for the last ten minutes. This secures it. At a bid of $400 million. With the commission and other additions, the buyer actually paid $450,312,500, the highest price ever paid for a work of art, hugely exceeding the previous highest *at auction* which was $179.4 million for Pablo Picasso's *Les Femmes d'Alger* on 11 May 2015. Interestingly, this was also sold at Christie's, New York, in the same room, by Pylkkanen, and had the same very slow bidding, often rising by only $1m a bid.

So why did the *Salvator* fetch such a high price? On the face of it, it is not the most engaging of pictures. Yes, it might have been in the possession of those "three English Kings" (might, see below), but this is surely not enough? No, the reason that the *Salvator* fetched such a price is down to one word – Leonardo. The *Salvator* was cleverly marketed as "the last Da Vinci", the last painting by Leonardo that is ever likely to come before an auction. Your last chance to buy a painting by the most iconic of Renaissance "geniuses". This chapter considers how we know that this painting, or any other, is by a particular artist – examining the curious world of the connoisseur and "the eye", an almost mystical sense that the best connoisseurs have, or claim to have, that tells them that an art work is "right". It also looks at how much of an artwork has to be painted by an artist for it to be by that artist and the related subject of the effect of conservation and restoration.

Leonardo Da Vinci was born in 1452 in Vinci, near Florence in Italy. He was educated in the studio of Andrea del Verrochio and spent much of his working life in the courts of patrons in Milan and later Rome, Bologna, Venice and eventually France. He has become renowned as the greatest of the Renaissance thinkers because in addition to his paintings, discussed below, he left hundreds of pages of notes and drawings detailing everything from engineering schemes for canals, flying machines, the internal workings of the human body, mapwork, siege engines, architecture, the list is endless. However, it is perhaps for his paintings that he is most known. The list of how many of his paintings have survived is hotly debated, but may stretch to twenty or so, some unfinished, all either religious scenes, often portraying the Virgin Mary, or courtly portraits.

((*I teach a class each year that looks at the value of paintings and why some are worth more than others. There are many factors, including artist, size, composition and so on. I ask the class to pick the five most famous paintings of all time and rank them in order. Over the years, perhaps a dozen paintings come up on a regular basis with artists such as Picasso (Guernica), Van Gogh (Sunflowers), Vermeer (Girl with the Pearl Earring – especially after the film of the same name came out) and Munch (Scream). However, only Leonardo routinely featured in two of the top spots. The first of these was for The Last Supper, strictly a fresco, but the remarkable one is of course Mona Lisa, which every group, in every class, every year, has placed first – the most famous painting ever. Very few of the students have seen it for real, but all can instantly identify it from a postcard. Why this is the most famous painting ever is very interesting. In the nineteenth century it would not have been; it seems only in the twentieth does it reach this status. This might partly be down to the fact that it was stolen in 1911 and lost for two and a half years before being returned. This was big news and hit newspapers across the world. The notoriety of the theft is part of the reason for its fame, along with some careful marketing by the Louvre. The painting* *travelled to the USA in the 1960s and thereafter to Tokyo and Moscow in the 1970s. It was seen by millions and the image was incorporated into the mind of the western world through posters, advertisements, postcards and latterly numerous television programmes. It is interesting to speculate on its value. For the USA tour it was assessed for insurance at $100 million, roughly $600 million in today's money. It is doubtful that the Mona Lisa will ever travel from its place in the Louvre again – without a very special reason and a fortune in security and insurance (plus the loss to the Louvre of its no.1 attraction being away). It will remain in Paris. However, the Mona Lisa's fame plays an important role in making Leonardo the most famous of artists and a role in the price paid for the* Salvator Mundi.

The *Salvator Mundi* easily fits into the Leonardo list of portraits and religious scenes. It is a subject that was widely painted at the time, and Leonardo's assistants and followers certainly painted copies of it. The key question is whether the *Salvator Mundi* sold at Christies is just another one of these copies or the original Leonardo which inspired the other works. How does one know that a painting is by Leonardo, or indeed any artist? The first consideration would be the idea of *provenance*.

We have talked elsewhere in this volume about provenance. It is a word that has two meanings in the overlapping world of art and antiques and the scientists who work on them. As discussed in the chapter on the Getty Kouros, to a scientist the provenance of an object is either where it was made, or perhaps more usually where the materials that the object is made of came from – in the Kouros case the "provenance" of the stone was the Thasos quarries of Greece. However, to most in the art world the provenance of an object is the history of that object from its manufacture to now, backed up by the names of those who have owned it, sales catalogues and receipts and scholarly works recording its importance. This was the material forged in the Getty Kouros case. In an ideal world the provenance documents would stretch in an unbroken line from the artist's studio to the current owner, each change of ownership carefully documented with receipts and catalogues of sale. Sometimes this is possible, especially with famous works that have been in the hands of royal collections or major aristocratic houses. However, mostly, especially for relatively early artists like Leonardo, this is not possible. So what can the provenance of the *Salvator Mundi* tell us about how likely it is that the painting is by Leonardo?

Well, the provenance of the *Salvator Mundi* is nothing if not spectacular. It is almost certainly the most extreme example of a "sleeper" that has ever been found, and probably ever will. In the art world, a "sleeper" is a work of art that has been mislabelled in some way so as to make it sell at a price that is far below that of its value if its true "identity" had been known. For we know for certain that the *Salvator* was sold at auction in April 2005. However, is was not in the plush surroundings of Christie's, New York. It was actually sold in a small provincial auction house in New Orleans, USA, called the St Charles Gallery. Here, rather than being placed between works of art that sell for millions, it was sold between a needlepoint panel (estimate $250-400) and a white marble figure (estimate $800-1,200). As lot 664 it is described as "After Leonardo da Vinci", and the description of the frame "Presented in a fine antique gilt and gesso exhibition frame" is almost as long as that for the rest of the picture, suggesting that the frame might be seen as a significant part of the value. There is a small, poor, black and white image in the catalogue; the painting was not considered important enough for colour plate, although the marble statue that followed it was. Estimated at $1,200-1,800, it just failed to reach its estimate and sold for $1,175. This means that in twelve years it went from selling for a little over a thousand dollars to a little over $450m. This means that the painting gained nearly $100,000 in value *every single day*. It is only by the power of connoisseurship, the gift of "the eye", that this was possible, to take what was virtually a junk lot at a no-name auction house and "recreate" it as the most expensive piece of art the world has ever known. How is this done?

❝ As with most people who work even peripherally in the art world, connoisseurs, good and bad, are a frequent part of my life. They are quite a variable group, from the overly flamboyant in silk scarves and red socks with their Savile Row suits, voicing their strident opinions to the world in general, to retiring scholarly types who are almost diffident in giving any information at all. They are, in my experience, mostly male, but this reflects history more than current practice and this has been noticeably shifting over the last decade or so. I have not worked with connoisseurs in the Old Master Painting field, but I have seen them and heard them working in art fairs such as TEFAF and Masterpiece. I have worked with connoisseurs in other specialist areas however, and it is an interesting experience. They will pick up a piece and prod it a little and relatively quickly they will come to a conclusion as to whether they "like it" or not – in other words whether it is a genuine piece or a later copy/forgery. I have tried to get one or two to justify their conclusions, and several things have become clear over the years of doing this. Firstly, they tend to come to a conclusion very quickly, usually in seconds. Occasionally they might change their minds on examining a piece in detail, but this is rare; the initial reaction almost always carries it. Asking them what they do not like about a piece is often not very instructive. They will talk about line, about the quality of brushwork, use of colour and composition, none of which is easily testable to a scientist. I often get the impression that they do not really know why they do not like certain pieces – they appear sometimes to be operating what to my mind is backwards – they come to their conclusion and then assemble evidence to support it. They seem to have a gut instinct whether a piece is "right" or not, something that they can attempt to deconstruct and explain, but it is deeper and more complicated than that. I have often wondered how this instinct comes about. Are they born with it or do they acquire it? I think it is a bit of both. Certainly, the best have their genetic instinct refined by decades of fine study of a wide range of objects that are in their area of expertise. This instinct, known as the *"eye", seems laughable perhaps to a scientist, but my experience is that, somewhat frustratingly, at the times when I have been able to "test" the eye with an independent analysis, it has almost always been right. It is worth remembering that the whole art world works this way. A very, very small number of objects are ever analysed or have bullet-proof provenance; with the rest it is down to someone telling you that the piece is what the piece looks to be – a connoisseur's eye.*

The *Salvator Mundi* was bought for a thousand dollars by Robert Simon and Alexander Parish, art dealers based near New York. Simon was more the scholar, with a doctorate in Art History from the University of Columbia, whereas Parish had long experience of handling paintings for auction houses and dealers, and in particular made his business in looking for undervalued art in modest salerooms across the USA. Their purchase of the *Salvator* was just one project that they had worked on together and they bought it thinking that they were buying a painting by "an artist associated with Leonardo". As far as can be made out, they did not see the painting in real life before they bought it. When they did see it, their "initial response was one of relief" that the painting was not a later copy, but did indeed seem to be "of the period", revealed by the quality of the blessing hand, hair and the decoration to the tunic. However, it had centuries of overpainting and restoration in other areas – they would need a specialist to determine what was period and what could be removed as later alterations. Simon turned to a colleague he had worked with before, Dianne Modestini. She was Director of the Kress Program in Painting Conservation at the Institute of Fine Art in New York and worked in private practice conserving and restoring. She cleaned the painting of dark varnishes and then went on to repair the panel that it was painted onto and removed the repaint and refill to old damage that was on large areas of it. She then went on to carefully repaint damaged areas so that the image would come together as a whole again, rather than the damage and poor early restoration dominating the painting.

Meanwhile, research went on into the provenance of the painting. How did it end up in an auction house in New Orleans? Slowly the story came together. The painting had been consigned to the auction house by the estate of a Louisianan sheet-metal contractor named Basil C. Hendry. However, markings on the back of the painting showed that it had previously been in the Cook Collection, and purchased for that collection in 1900 from Sir John Charles Robinson, who had bought it at Christie's where it was consigned by the estate of the "Late Joseph Hirst", a Leeds cloth merchant. The tracing of the painting earlier than this becomes complex, but a key piece of evidence rested in the collection of the office of the Surveyor of The Queen's Pictures in St James Palace in London. This was an inventory of pictures owned by King Charles II at Whitehall and Hampton Court, produced in the mid-1660s. Listed at number 311 and held "in the King's Closet" is "Leonard de Vince. O^r Savio^r wth a gloabe in one hand and holding up ye other". This firmly places a *Salvator* painting, thought to be by Leonardo, in the Royal collection in the middle of the seventeenth century. The obvious question remains, is the painting in the inventory Simon's painting, or is it another *Salvator*? As discussed, there were many copies in the style of Leonardo. The exhaustive research initiated by Simon suggests that they are the same, but others remain unconvinced, showing that there are many mentions of *Salvator*s in collections at the time.

The debate over the *Salvator* goes on. Almost all agree that the painting is "of the period"; in other words it dates from the time of Leonardo or shortly thereafter. All agree that the painting depicts Christ as *Salvator*, and that Leonardo painted such a picture, which was venerated and copied by other artists but was subsequently lost. All agree that the painting was damaged and has been restored repeatedly over the centuries. There is therefore only one questions that remains unanswered – is this the lost Leonardo or another copy of that painting by an assistant or follower? Unfortunately, as we have discussed above, science is not going to help greatly in answering this question. Science can analyse the paints, but it is unlikely that this will tell us more than that this picture is "of the period", which we already know. It can image the painting and look at underdrawing, retouching or changes to the composition, but without someone to interpret what this means with respect to the painting, this information is of incidental interest only. What is needed is an expert on the period and the painting of Leonardo, and there are several of these. The most important for this story is Martin Kemp, Emeritus Professor of the History of Art at Oxford University. Kemp has written numerous books on Leonardo and is regarded by many as one of the leading Leonardo scholars of the day. His scholarly works have added much to the understanding of Leonardo and his works, and his opinion on a disputed work carries much weight in the field. Kemp became a key player in the rehabilitation and eventual sale of the *Salvator*. He was involved in a remarkable exhibition which was to present the painting to the World in general.

Robert Simon showed the painting to the National Gallery in London, specifically to the new Director, Nicholas Penny, and the curator, Luke Syson. They were planning a large Leonardo exhibition, and were intrigued by the idea that the *Salvator* might be included in that. This would be unusual, since national museums and galleries do not normally want to be seen advertising privately owned paintings that might conceivably be on sale in the future. However, any reservations on this were overcome, partly by Simon agreeing to a independent assessment of the painting by a panel of connoisseurs at the National Gallery, including Martin Kemp. The panel of five Leonardo experts met in late 2008, and viewed the painting next to the National Gallery's version of the *Virgin of the Rocks*. It was the first time that Kemp had seen the painting, and he and others have made public comments on the panel's work. Kemp was interviewed by the art website Blouin Artinfo and talked about his initial reaction, which conveys something of that feeling that the best connoisseurs have about the works that they authenticate. He said, "It had that kind of presence that Leonardos have. The *Mona Lisa* has a presence. So after that initial reaction, which is kind of almost inside your body, as it were, you look at it and you think, well, the handling of the better-preserved parts, like the hair and so on, is just incredibly good. It's got that kind of uncanny vortex, as if the hair is a living, moving substance, or like water, which is what Leonardo said hair was like". An initial gut reaction is key. A second member of the panel, art historian Professor Pietro Marani (who distinguished himself by supervising a widely praised restoration of Leonardo's *The Last Supper*), also had an immediate reaction. Talking to the *Daily Mail*, he said, "we could tell at once that it was a work by da Vinci". Others seemed less sure, and in the end the meeting did not come to a universal opinion as to whether the painting was by Leonardo. Indeed, to a certain extent, that was not the aim of the meeting, and presumably that was not what the National Gallery was after. Syson was clear in discussion with Ben Lewis that "it was about gauging opinion and seeing if we were going to expose ourselves to ridicule. If everyone had said clearly 'This isn't him,' then we would not have shown it". The consensus was that Leonardo had been involved in the depiction of parts of the painting, interestingly, the parts that most stand out to the untrained eye too (as discussed above), especially the blessing hand and the crystal orb. The damage to large areas of the painting meant it was difficult for some to say more.

In November 2011, the National Gallery's Leonardo Exhibition opened. Entitled "Leonardo da Vinci: Painter at the Court of Milan", it was one of the hottest tickets in London at the time and sold out almost immediately. Over six rooms, more than half of the fifteen or so paintings universally agreed to be by Leonardo alone were on display, alongside drawings, cartoons and other works. The *Salvator* was included, catalogue no. 71. It is interesting to note that while the authorship of other works in the exhibition was described with all the circumspect caution you would expect (Nos. 56 and 57 "After Leonardo da Vinci"; No.63 "Follower of Leonardo da Vinci"; No.72 "Leonardo da Vinci and workshop"), the *Salvator* is simply "Leonardo da Vinci", so in the catalogue it received the same "billing" as incontrovertible autograph works such as the Louvre's *Virgin of the Rocks*. This will not have harmed the value of the painting, and its presence in a National Gallery exhibition of this stature very much helped to legitimise it. It is no accident that the first words of the text of the extensive Christie's catalogue discussed above are:

> "The dramatic public unveiling of the *Salvator Mundi* ('Saviour of the World') in the exhibition *Leonard da Vinci: Painter at the Court of Milan* at The National Gallery, London, in 2011, caused a worldwide sensation".

The work by Kemp, and more indirectly the other connoisseurs and The National Gallery, while not generating anywhere near a consensus on the picture, was enough to improve the value of the picture by $100k a day. This is an extreme case of the effect of connoisseurship, but the effect applies to almost all objects sold on the art market – a powerful force. It is not unusual for connoisseurs to disagree. Indeed, this is as true of the Leonardo scholars as any other. Many of the scholars had particular favourites that they thought were by Leonardo, or aspects of the painting that were by Leonardo. It was common that these favourites were not accepted by the others. An important example of this was Kemp's championing of *La Bella Principessa*, a chalk and ink drawing on vellum of a young girl in profile in a Renaissance-style dress.

The certain provenance of *La Bella Principessa* stretches only to 1998, when it was sold at Christie's as Lot 402 of their Old Master Drawings auction. It is described there as "German School, early 19ᵗʰ Century" and sold for $21,850. The seller believed that it had been in their family since 1955, before which there is no certain link to earlier evidence. It was sold again soon afterwards and then, in 2007, Peter Silverman, an art dealer, spotted it in a gallery in New York and wondered whether it could be older than the date attributed to it. Just as with the *Salvator*, Silverman consulted the connoisseurs to find their opinion, and prominent among them, again, was Martin Kemp. Once again, Kemp co-authored a book on the subject, authenticating *La Bella Principessa* as a work by Leonardo. Some of the same techniques spotted in the *Salvator* are also present in *La*

Bella Principessa and link it to Leonardo. His opinion, however, has been far less well received by the Leonardo community than his view of the *Salvator*, and *La Bella Principessa* still remains a questioned work. Most noticeably, it was not included in the National Gallery Exhibition, although it would have been ideal for it. Apparently, the National Gallery did not ask for it to be loaned to them. Despite this, newspaper reports valued Silverman's drawing at in excess of $100 million, and that was in the early 2010s, before the *Salvator* reached its record price. A final, delicious twist in the tail comes from (of all places) Bolton in Northern England. As recounted in other chapters (see Amarna Princess), a prolific forger named Shaun Greenhalgh was working in a variety of media, and published his memoires in a book entitled *A Forger's Tale*. In it Greenhalgh claims that he produced *La Bella Principessa*. He says, "I drew this picture in 1978 when I worked at the Co-op. The 'sitter' was based on a girl called Sally who worked on the check outs". For once, he gives some details about how he did it – how and where he got the vellum, how he prepared it, what drawings he used and the colours chosen. It is interesting that there is more here about how he carried out the deed than with almost any other work that he is definitely known to have produced. He then goes on to critique his own work, point-ing out the mistakes that he claims to have made. He even has a direct dig at Kemp, saying, "Although I am no Oxford professor, I could list umpteen reasons for not thinking this drawing to be by Leonardo". Despite widespread joyous reporting from the press ("It's not a da Vinci, it's Sally from the Co-op", *The Times*, 29 November 2015), it is not widely believed that Greenhalgh produced *La Bella Principessa. However,* as discussed above, it is not widely thought to be a Leonardo either. Martin Kemp's reputation has therefore not been affected by Greenhalgh's claims, and his opinion on *La Bella Principessa* remains.

There are several cases of world experts being fooled by talented or fortunate fakers. One of the most disastrous for the celebrated connoisseur involved was the "Hitler Diaries" scandal. Hugh Trevor-Roper was a celebrated student at Oxford in the 1930s, winning prizes for examinations in Classics before changing to History and taking a first class degree. He was destined for an academic career before the Second World War got in the way. He joined the Army and went on to work in various intelligence roles. Soon after the end of the War, he was asked by British Intelligence to investigate the circumstances of Hitler's death, specifically to put to rest wild stories that Hitler was still alive somewhere. He did this with great diligence, and out of this work came a volume that was released for public sale in 1947, "The Last Days of Hitler". This clearly and comprehensively proved that Hitler was dead, but incidentally made Trevor-Roper an expert on Hitler, and he would be regarded as such for the rest of his life, despite writing on many other areas of history. After the War he returned to Oxford and rose to be Regius Professor of Modern History and ennobled to be Lord Dacre of Glanton, before moving to be Master of Peterhouse, Cambridge, in 1980. He gave advice in several high-profile fakes and forgeries cases, but the most significant occurred in 1983, soon after he arrived in Cambridge. The German magazine *Stern* was offered 60 volumes that claimed to be the diaries of Adolf Hitler. They bought the diaries and sold serialisation rights to several newspapers including the *Sunday Times*. Dacre, as he now was, was asked to verify their authenticity and wrote a long article for the sister paper, *The Times*, discussing their importance. However, he quickly began to have doubts about whether the Diaries were right and then changed his mind completely. Despite this, the *Sunday Times* went ahead and published substantial extracts from them in a much-trumpeted major article that was to run over several weeks. Forensic tests on the ink used showed that it was very likely modern and that it had been written in the last couple of years, not in the 1940s. Investigation subsequently showed that all 60 volumes of the Diaries had actually been written by a Konrad Kujau, a dealer in Nazi memorabilia who collected material in East Germany and sold it in the West. He found that he could improve the value of objects if they were associated with a senior Nazi official. Even more so if they bore the signature of such an official. The *Hitler Diaries* were his *magnum opus*, but he had made clear errors in the works, and Dacre was initially taken in and the Diaries were published at least in part because of Dacre's initially positive reaction to them.

The result for Dacre was catastrophic. He was made a laughingstock, and his reputation was badly damaged. As the Guardian's obituary reads, it was "the gravest of those errors of overconfidence to which he was occasionally prone". He was not helped in the reaction to this revelation by his somewhat acerbic criticism of other people's work, which had not made him friends. Now in this rare, but major error, those he had criticised had an ideal opportunity to score a few points back. Nearly all obituaries written for Dacre (he died in 2003) mention this Diaries scandal as a low point – it haunted him for the rest of his life. The *Guardian* obituary writer sees him as a changed man after the incident, believing that the "humiliation contributed to [his] mellowing, and to the growing tendency to self-deprecation, that grew conspicuous in his later years. His prose yielded something of its exuberance and assertiveness, though none of its elegance or suppleness or wit". A beautiful way of phrasing it.

So a connoisseur is a powerful thing to be. Those at the top of their game can change objects worth thousands into objects worth many, many millions. They do this by dint of their decades of study of the subject matter, but even more by some sort of innate sense of how the artist worked, and what they would have produced. They often know immediately if something is "right", although they will then go on to justify their gut instinct with detailed analysis. However, it is also a risky thing to be. As Douglas Fairbanks might have said, they are "only as good as their last picture". In other words, one mistake could bring their reputation crashing down. There is nothing the press likes more than finding an art expert who has authenticated a valuable fake – and it does happen.

Chapter 8
The Reconstruction of Knossos

"…unusualness was the essence of his being":
Dame Joan Evans on Sir Arthur Evans in 1943

In the chapter on Leonardo we considered when an object, in this case specifically a painting, could be called an autograph work of the artist. Specifically, how much input into a painting is needed? Does the artist have to paint it all, or part, or is it enough that it was in the artist's studio and s/he gave advice to a student on how to proceed with it? This led on to the whole problem of attribution when a painting has, according to the connoisseur, been the product of multiple hands – how much Leonardo makes a painting a "Leonardo"? Here we consider a parallel question, which was mentioned in passing in that chapter. What happens if an object is damaged and repaired? Early paintings in our most famous galleries have almost all been significantly repainted. This has been done throughout their history, their object biography – and is still done today. However, what if that subsequent work hides or corrupts the original work? How much restoration could there be before an object is no longer the object, and essentially becomes a modern replica?

There was a very popular television comedy shown throughout the 1980s in the UK called *Only Fools and Horses*. It is still loved by millions and can easily be found on the internet. In a classic episode, one of the characters, Trigger (a road sweeper), is awarded a medal for looking after his broom – he says he has had "the same broom for the last twenty years". His friends are surprised, because they know that he has used the broom every day in his work. However, he has cared for it, he says he has "maintained it for twenty years. This old broom has had 17 new heads and 14 new handles in its time". Which leads to huge laughter and the obvious comment, "How the hell can it be the same bloody broom then?".

A view of the Knossos archaeological site, the western part of the "North Entrance" ("Northern Bastion") of the palace of Knossos, a major national asset accessible to tourists.
Picture by Jan Driessen. © Hellenic Ministry of Culture and Sports (N. 3028/2002).

A detail of the reconstruction and restoration works at Knossos,
view of the "Northern Purification Tank", where it becomes unclear
what was the original archaeological structure excavated,
and what has been "reconstituted".
Picture by Gavin McGuire. © Hellenic Ministry of Culture and Sports
(N. 3028/2002).

As often with these British comedies, the writing is not only funny, but rather clever. The idea behind this joke touches on arguments more fundamental and interesting than they might seem and a debate that has gone on for millennia. The question is the same as that posed at the beginning of this chapter: how much of an object needs to remain for that object to be that object? This subject was first debated by the ancient philosophers, perhaps back to Plato in *Paramenides*. The essence of the argument is first spelled out in print by Plutarch, or at least that is the earliest surviving account we have of it. It is sometimes known as the "Ship of Theseus Paradox":

"The ship wherein Theseus and the youth of Athens returned had thirty oars, and was preserved by the Athenians down even to the time of Demetrius Phalereus, for they took away the old planks as they decayed, putting in new and stronger timber in their place, insomuch that this ship became a standing example among the philosophers, for the logical question of things that grow; one side holding that the ship remained the same, and the other contending that it was not the same"
Plutarch (*Vita Thesei*, 22-23)

The essence of the question is that over time the ship is slowly replaced. Does this make it any less Theseus's ship? When does what is left cease to be Theseus's ship: after the first piece is removed? After the last piece of the original is removed? Somewhere in between? Or, as with Trigger's broom, is it always Theseus's ship even if it is all replaced, all new? In this idea, something of the essence of the identity of the ship and broom persists after the material component has been replaced. It might seem obvious that the ship cannot be Theseus's ship when no material component of that ship is left. However, in a more modern twist to the tail, what if Theseus repairs his ship during his voyage, such that it is completely replaced while he is on board? Is this then a new ship or is it Theseus's ship? It seems clearer here that it is still Theseus's ship, so there are subtleties involved. Another example often cited to criticise the "only the material component matters" philosophy is the idea of a river. A river remains the same river to us, even though the material component of that river (the water) is continually changing and never the same again. This leads to another idea, that all things are changing continually, so that the material component is less important – Trigger's broom, like a river, is still the same broom.

These concepts feed into a fundamental problem faced by those who study, curate and care for historical objects. Almost by definition, historical objects will have been subject to wear and deterioration, and hence will not be completely pristine, as they were the day that they were made. Many will have damaged or even missing parts. What should be done about this? Should parts be repaired and replaced? Should every effort be made to make the object look like it did the moment it was made? Alternatively, should the damage be left and not replaced? There is a concept that most (but not all) would agree with, and that might be termed "conservation". Conservation might be taken as the prevention of an object deteriorating further. This is a fundamental role of nearly all museums, to keep their objects safe for future generations. This conservation might be entirely passive – keeping the objects in the right conditions in terms of heat and humidity, supporting them and wrapping them correctly in storage and handling them as little as possible. However, it might be more active – degradation might be removed to stop it developing further, protective coatings might be applied. However, we will often want to go further. If an object is broken, the next stage in conservation might be to reassemble it. Here we are moving slowly down the track towards "restoration", the returning of an object to a previous state or, in its most extreme form, a new state. How far a museum goes down the track towards restoration is a cultural decision, either for the museum itself or for the wider academic community. Perhaps strangely, different decisions are often made, even within one museum, depending on the object type. Some examples help to illustrate the problems and decisions that have to be made.

To start with a relatively simple example, a pot recovered from the excavation broken into sherds might be stuck back together for museum display. Very few museums would argue with this approach if it is done in a reversable way. However, what to do if there are sherds missing? They could simply be left as holes, but that might affect the vessel structurally and make it too delicate to display. Another solution is to fill the holes to restore the vessel to its original shape. However, this would still make the repair obvious, so should the infills be coloured? If they are, should they be a close match, so that from a distance the vessel has the appearance of the original but close up the repair is obvious, or should it aim to look completely like the original, even close up? Should the cracks between sherds be similarly repaired and hidden? In the past, many museums have gone through the entire process here and produced objects that have looked complete, even when they were not. This is still the policy of many collectors and dealers – clients want objects that look complete. However, western museums have now to a great extent changed their policy on this. Now, archaeological objects in particular tend to be left with the damage obvious, at least close up. However, other objects, especially paintings, are routinely repaired and touched up to make damage invisible, at least to the casual viewer and often to the expert as well. There seems to be a difference in attitude between those who see objects as archaeological and those who see them as art. Art museums are much more likely to repair objects and will typically move further down the restoration track than archaeology museums will. They sometimes argue that their customers are interested in different aspects of the objects, and those aspects are enhanced by the object being as close to the complete as possible – people's attitude towards "art" is badly affected by damage and decay in a way that their attitude to archaeology is not. Other museums outside Europe and America again have a different attitude and will frequently restore when they can, even at the expense of removing some of the original object to make this possible – this is particularly the case with restoring historical buildings. Buildings, or all historical artefacts, still need to "function" in at least some of their original roles. This can make them especially interesting in highlighting attitudes to restoration. However, it is important to note that there is no "right" or "wrong" here, just different approaches to how historical material should be treated.

The rest of this chapter will consider the preservation of not just an object or even a building, but of a site. To take a very well-known example, consider Stonehenge. This is a world heritage site dating to the second millennium BCE in Southern England. Famous for the huge stones used, it is incomplete, with stones lying where they have fallen and many stones missing. In the past, stones have been put back into place at Stonehenge, others straightened to stop them toppling over. However, should the missing stones be replaced? This would be a very large task, and require a degree of interpretation – where actually were the stones and how did they look? While it might be preferable to replace missing stones with stone of the same type, it would be easier to do this with concrete. Should the missing stones be replaced with concrete pseudo stones? Obviously, this is never going to happen. It would never be allowed under the rules of Historic England, who run the site. However, consider a site of similar antiquity and importance where just such a process was carried out – Knossos.

Knossos

To excavate the remains of a culture long lost, was the childhood dream of many who became archaeologists, and it is an ongoing fantasy for many who didn't. On your next holiday, should you ever want to dream and at the same time see the impact archaeological sites can make on local tourism development, the Mediterranean is-land of Crete is an excellent place to go. On the outskirts of the local capital of Heraklion lies an attraction drawing thousands of people a day. Quite surprising, if you judge by the width of the road leading there. The ancient site of Knossos is one of the biggest tourist draws on the island, a major attraction. But do not worry about parking, food or drink – all is foreseen!

For Sir Arthur Evans, the dream of finding a civilisation de-scribed only in legend became reality. Educated at the universities of Oxford and Göttingen, Arthur Evans in 1884 became a keeper at the Ashmolean Museum at Oxford University, a post he held until he was appointed Professor of Prehistoric Archaeology at Oxford in 1908. Between 1900 and 1905 he excavated the 'Palace of Knossos'. This citadel belonged to a civilisation that Evans named the "Minoans", after the mythical Cretan King Minos (though we cannot be sure what this civilisation called itself). The excavations at Knossos suddenly made this people, known only from some ancient texts and the Bible, very real. The quick and mysterious destruction of Minoan culture all around the Mediterranean, by some attributed to a tsunami following the violent eruption of the Thera volcano in the seventeenth to sixteenth centuries BCE, has often been cited as the basis for the legend of Atlantis. The myth of the labyrinth at Knossos, holding the terrible half-man, half-bull Minotaur, killed by Theseus who escapes the labyrinth using Minos' daughter Ariadne's thread, is known to almost all. The real Minoans were a people of influence and power, and this is reflected in the wealth and grandeur of the complex found at Knossos.

Evans wasn't actually the first to find the archaeological remains at Knossos. In 1878 and 1879, the Cretan antiquarian Minos Kalokairinos excavated parts of Kephala Hill, where the palace was built, but was stopped by the Ottoman authorities. Subsequently, the legendary German archaeologist Heinrich Schliemann, excavator at Troy, briefly dug at the site. His sudden death in 1890 put a stop to his plans for further work at Knossos. As a keeper of the Ashmolean, even before himself excavating in Crete, Evans acquired around 2,000 objects per year for the museum, expanding its archaeological collections substantially. The Ashmolean to this day houses the most important collection of Aegean artefacts outside Greece, owing to purchases and pioneering excavations in the region by a number of celebrated Oxford scholars. Sir Arthur's merits in obtaining this collection are still celebrated in the Ashmolean Museum today. He travelled to Greece several times in the 1880s and 90s, and for instance met with the Schliemann in Athens in 1883. His efforts in expanding the collections also aroused his interests in early writing in pre-Classical Greece. Having seen seals with symbols engraved on them coming from sales in Athens, and knowing of more to be found in Crete, Evans visited the island for the first time in 1894.

In 1899, Evans bought the Kephala Hill site from the newly declared autonomous state of Crete for an undisclosed sum. Evans' father, Sir John, had made his fortune in paper mills and was a self-taught archaeologist in whose footsteps Arthur followed. Sir John funded his son's expeditions in Crete substantially, in total to an estimated amount of £250,000. This allowed archaeological work which would last until 1929-1930. In the early years of the twentieth century, a wealthy individual could do with a site very much as they pleased. Local or international regulations were lacking and academic credentials or scrutiny often deemed unnecessary. Nevertheless, as a professional archaeologist, Evans excavated with due diligence and was a perfect fit for the site. On 23 March 1900 work started, and within a few weeks hundreds of clay tablets inscribed with early writing were discovered. Over the years, Evans was to find evidence of three scripts on Crete. The first is pictographic or hieroglyph, showing pictorials representing phonetic sounds rather than what is shown in the picture. The other two are Linear A and Linear B, two scripts made up of lines and much less pictorial. Of these, only Linear B has been deciphered, Michael Ventris showing in 1952 that it was an archaic form of ancient Greek. The hieroglyph script and Linear A still remain a mystery, and probably represent languages entirely unrelated to Greek.

Excavations in the early 1900s by Evans showed the Knossos palace to be a complex of more than a thousand chambers around a central courtyard, branching out into several wings along the north-south and east-west axes, with entrances in all directions. Sanctuaries, formal halls and storage spaces are situated in the west wing, while the Royal Apartments can be found in the east wing. Workshops, warehouses and other functional buildings can be found in the north and south wings. The structure displays the most sophisticated architectural techniques of its time, building several stories high, including a water management system for the supply of fresh water and a drainage system for run off and waste water. The very maze-like nature of the complex is what prompted Evans to give the Minoans their name, after the legend of King Minos, the Minotaur and the mythical labyrinth.

From further excavations and archaeological research it has become clear that the site of Knossos in fact shows evidence of occupation from around 7000 BCE, and many generations lived and built there atop one another. What is known as the first "palace" structure must have been completed around 1900 BCE and destroyed around

1700 BCE. A second palace stood on the same location until what most scholars consider to be 1375 BCE, when this structure burnt down and marked the end of the palace culture. Subsequent peoples inhabited the site in private homes up to the late Roman period, around the fifth century CE.

Other Minoan palaces have been excavated on Crete, but Knossos remains the largest and most important. Interestingly, these complexes were not military in nature, as no fortifications or weapon stores have ever been identified. Their function must have been administrative-political or religious-ceremonial, but most likely both. The Minoans boasted a society with seemingly great social and gender equality and a remarkably even distribution of wealth. They traded with the peoples of the Near East and Egypt, and worshipped their own gods and goddesses with symbols such as the bull and the double-sided axe. Beautiful frescos and carvings at Knossos, of which many originals are kept at the local Heraklion museum, featured seemingly ageless men and women practising sports or the arts.

Evans was knighted in King George V's coronation honours in 1911 for his services to archaeology, and his name is one of the legends of the discipline. However, one aspect of his work at Knossos remains controversial, to put things mildly. The Ashmolean display on Aegean culture states that "through his lectures, publications and exhibitions, Evans dominated the field for almost half a century and shaped our understanding of Minoan Crete. His extensive reconstructions at Knossos, a matter of great controversy even in his own time, remain the most visible testimony of his visions of the past". In the Ashmolean display, a painting by Sir William Richmond can be seen, made in 1907, showing Evans holding a tablet of Linear B in a Cretan setting. In the background is a "freely interpreted reconstruction of the ruins of Knossos". On Crete, present-day visitors to Knossos can see the structure of the palace and the maze of interconnected spaces, admire the earliest throne room in Europe and see many colourful wall paintings. All of these, however, are the result of extensive, usually contested, and sometimes even damaging reconstruction. Sir Arthur led these restorations, which he himself called "reconstitutions".

To help preserve the archaeological remains that have been revealed, some archaeologists backfill what they have excavated with the material that was initially removed. However, when trenches, graves or remains of architecture are left open, conservation measures have to be taken. If left exposed to the elements, most archaeological features will not survive long. Evans believed that the palace of Knossos could be revived in its glory of old, but the site was recreated in a substantial part following Evans' personal "vision", not necessarily based on solid archaeological knowledge or, in this case, even reality. The reconstructed Palace of Knossos is in fact one of the first reinforced concrete buildings erected on Crete, often covering original parts of the structure in the process, and damaging archaeological features. The rebuilding and re-interpretation of the site eventually led to it receiving the doubtful title of the "Disneyland of archaeology".

Restoration of the Knossos architectural remains began almost immediately after the first excavations. Three phases in this work can be distinguished, each with its own philosophy devised by the architect who led the works. As the winter of 1900 had damaged the freshly excavated Throne Room, Evans hired Theodore Fyfe as the architect to lead the first five years of restoration and conservation at Knossos. Fyfe approached the site with the idea that minimal intervention was advised, and that only materials authentic to the Bronze Age could be used. He was clearly concerned with the truthfulness of his reconstructions, except for the roof structures he set up to protect areas such as the Throne Room. This approach, however, failed: the use of authentic materials such as untreated wood or gypsum, unadjusted to the exposed situation, soon saw the restoration works in need of their own conservation. As of 1905, Fyfe was replaced by Christian Doll. He repaired Fyfe's work, and was responsible for the stabilisation and reconstruction of the originally four-storey-high Grand Staircase. The exact design of this structure, however, was unknown and much improvisation and imagination were necessary in its rebuilding. Doll introduced contemporary materials to the site, as the authentic approach of Fyfe had failed, and used iron girders, cement and concrete in a modern structural design.

Most of the reconstruction work, in effect most of what Knossos looks like today, was rebuilt between 1922 and 1952, led by Dutch-English architect and artist Piet de Jong. Lacking any archaeological training, he reconstructed the site beyond what was known from excavation, drawn by himself often based on reconstructions imagined by Evans. They gave the site a picturesque vision rather than a historically correct one. De Jong prominently used iron reinforced concrete, a cheap and malleable material that was thought to be nearly indestructible. The reconstruction of the Throne Room as it is today, for instance, displays a combination of archaeological knowledge from excavation, the creativity of Evans and the romantic view of de Jong. Wooden columns and beams were reconstructed from concrete and rendered colour. Also, the reproductions of wall paintings in these newly built spaces are an addition by de Jong, helped by the designs of Emile Gilliéron the Younger, a Swiss artist and archaeological illustrator. Some frescoes were placed close to their original find spot and are authentic to the excavated remains, but others, perhaps most, have no connection to the actual archaeology of the site. Already in 1926, the president of the Society of Antiquaries expressed his concern over the confusion that would occur in the near future, when what was original and what was reconstructed would no longer be entirely clear.

The reconstruction at Knossos has merit in that it recreates a version of Minoan life in a way the original, excavated ruins never could. The Ashmolean Museum quotes Dame Joan Evans, Sir Arthur's half-sister, as saying that "the didactic streak in his nature – to make Knossos intelligible to other men" was what prompted him to these reconstructions "exceeding the practical necessity to protect and preserve the ruins from the elements". In general, archaeological restorations offer the visitor a clearer insight into and easier historical understanding of an ancient site. Had Evans not worked to preserve Knossos from the beginning of his excavations, all architectural remains would undoubtedly, and very quickly, have been lost. Nevertheless, what is shown now reflects Evans' very personal vision of the Bronze Age, an opinion which we now know is not a very accurate depiction of what the site once looked like. Moreover, the floorplan of what is presented today is mostly the later Mycenaean construction of the site, not the Minoan one. The site leaves the visitor the impression that there was only one Bronze Age site there, and visually neglects all other remains or history of the location, one layer superimposed or mixed with the other. While such information is displayed in text on site, it is often overlooked by visiting tourists. Also, the frescoes of Emile Gilliéron the Younger and his father, with their vivid and colourful designs, have undoubtedly shaped what we think of Minoan art today, but this is not archaeological or scientific reality.

Thus, should an excavated site ever be fully reconstructed to what we believe it looked like, according to the current state of scientific knowledge? Additionally, for a site with a long occupation history, which specific point in time do we then reconstruct? But if such choice is made, how will future changes in knowledge about a site then be accommodated? Which criteria are used to decide whether a site should be reconstructed at all?

The 1964 UNESCO Venice Charter is an international agreement on the conservation of historic buildings. The Charter states that the reconstruction of archaeological sites is to be avoided, and only anastylosis can be permitted. "Anastylosis" literally means "to re-erect a column" and is taken to mean the reassembling of a monument using its existing but dismembered parts. This process strictly requires that, when reinstated, each building member is used in its original position and structural function. This means that in this type of reconstruction of collapsed ancient structures, each scattered building block has to be identified, individually repaired and positioned in its original place, making this process a very effective conservation measure: a building and its separate components will deteriorate much less when in a complete structure. Moreover, when anastylosis is the product of meticulous research and architectural study it constitutes a learning process for a variety of sciences. The process is bound, though, by very strict criteria. Whether anastylosis of a monument is possible at all should be carefully considered. A well-documented excavation from the beginning of the project is essential. Collapsed, dispersed building fragments should be registered most accurately throughout the layers of the excavation (called the stratigraphy) for one to be able to puzzle the monument back together, with all constituents in their correct place. Excavating the immediate surroundings of a building is often also necessary for one to be able to place it in the right urban context or landscape. Also, the recovery of a high number of original building elements, often set at 80 to 90% of all components, is quintessential. Missing information on any aspect of the original structure leads to hypothetical reconstruction, and such conjecture is totally ruled out by the UNESCO convention. The fact that reliable restitution of the monument is possible with the available original material and the archaeological evidence at hand is the most important criterion for a restoration project to go ahead. Also, obviously, the reconstruction must be structurally sound. Conservation and consolidation of the building elements is necessary, but it should be evaluated whether structural issues can be rectified without intrusive modern intervention. The condition in which the original building materials are found determines whether they can be used or not. If certain elements are to be replaced by modern replicas, suitable material true to the nature of the original building has to be used, not only for aesthetic reasons, but more because modern and ancient materials will react differently to the outside environment and may be damaging to one another. This is a process called differential deterioration. Additionally, all modern conservation principles have reversibility as a central principle: all restorations must be non-destructive and reversible. The original remains must be left unharmed by restoration methods and materials, at the same time leaving open the option for more qualitative, less invasive conservation or a different interpretation-reconstruction in the future. Thus, conservation and restoration need to take into account the evolving scholarship around history, archaeology and engineering.

Even if anastylosis is possible, restoration at archaeological sites nowadays should always be carefully considered, and not just in terms of financial impact. Conservation science has moved away from merely the physical preservation of archaeological remains towards the sustainable management of cultural heritage. The reconstruction of a monument and the public relations and tourism income it provides are now seen in balance with the significance of a site and the wider landscape it belongs to. This comprises an adequate assessment by various experts of the special scientific value of a monument versus its contemporary symbolic, cultural, political and economic value. Moreover, while anastylosis constitutes an effective conservation measure, it may create a focal point of attraction physically dominating a site, overshadowing all other remains present.

It is likely that none of the criteria required by the Venice Charter would have been met at Knossos. Conversely, the fact that the Knossos site was abandoned for eight years during and after the First World War, in which all but the roof-covered remains suffered a great deal of damage, may be an understandable explanation for why Evans opted for the radical reconstruction strategy offered by de Jong, using inexpensive materials that could be quickly applied. In his 1875 memoirs, "Troy and its Remains", Heinrich Schliemann writes, "if my memoirs now and then contain contradictions, I hope that these may be pardoned when it is considered that I have here revealed a new world for archaeology". This holds true for Sir Arthur Evans and his reconstitutions as well. He envisaged the Knossos site to be open to future visitors, and wanted the culture he had discovered to be clearly explained to all. He bequeathed all his records, sketches and papers to the Ashmolean Museum upon his death in 1941. The museum shows photos and daybooks of the progress of the excavations, displays the reconstruction drawings of the site and has a mock-up of the Throne Room. The restorations at Knossos are discussed for what they are: controversial, and they should be seen in their own historical framework. Evans was convinced of the unicity and importance of the site, and was well aware from his Ashmolean background how connected knowledge of Minoan culture would be to the presentation of the site. Knossos was to be a museum and an open classroom, and is in fact the earliest example of cultural tourism with an impact on public education and local economy.

Since the Second World War further conservation work has been carried out at Knossos. Today it actually focusses on safeguarding the original remains, but also on repairing de Jong's reconstructions. His reinforced concrete has proven not to last and is crumbling. Moreover, tourist traffic over the past decades has put an enormous strain on both the archaeological remains and the reconstructions. Close to 100,000 visitors passed through the site in May 2018. Knossos is the most visited site in Crete, the second most visited archaeological site in Greece, and one of the most frequented in the world. Tourist traffic not only sustains the local economy, but also fuels an ever-continuing cycle of conservation works, balancing the protection of the monument with opening it to the wider public.

> ❝ When I visited the site, it became clear that Evans' restorations are absolutely dominant, and are the cause of more than a bit of confusion. Recent conservation works have minimised direct contact with the monument, both original and reconstituted, through the construction of wooden walkways, the outline of predetermined visitor paths and by cordoning off areas, making them inaccessible to the public. Even to the trained eye and from a distance it is not very clear what is archaeological and what is modern, and whether archaeological elements are in their original position. For me, this puts strain on the experience. But what about the average tourist?

Esther Solomon in the early 2000s studied visitors' experiences and expectations on site. People want to meet with the authentic, and see the local way of life on the island as it was thousands of years ago, as part of this enlightened, well-organised society. This is completely in line with the expressed intent of Arthur Evans' reconstructions. However, the reconstitutions as they are presented do have an immense influence on people's perception of Minoan Crete. Solomon gives the example of the trees planted by Evans to give a proper context for the palace, framing the Minoans' relationship with nature. Many visitors see this forest as a pleasant remains of a very old past, not as modern. Interestingly, when visitors are informed about the existing controversies over the reconstructions, they tend to be very critical of them. Their experience of the site is then judged in a less positive way, as if they are cheated in their personal experience of the site.

Knossos today is a source of national pride and a symbol for Crete. Even more, it is literally an emblem for modern products, and part of everyday life. Only by virtue of Sir Arthur Evans' efforts in conservation and reconstruction does the Knossos site still exist today. But people do not feel positive when informed of the fact that this image of an ancient society that lived in harmony with its environment is idealised, and not a real or true representation from scientific fact. People want to see the authentic. It raises the question of when a whole site is seen as authentic. All other chapters have considered the problem of authenticity around objects, but such interpretation for whole sites is more difficult. Apart from cultural heritage preservation criteria such as the ones stated by UNESCO, how many pieces of a site need to be original for one to *feel* it as real? When does imaginative restoration become "Disneyfication" and is a whole archaeological or cultural site perceived as a fake? It is clear that the impact of an alternative reconstruction (or the misinterpretation of scientific fact) on tourists, collectors and even the general public is immediate. Such an effect is not to be underestimated: unsubstantiated views of the past, be it on the scale of single objects to whole sites, can effectively lessen the value attributed to the interaction with an object, devalue personal or group cultural experiences, even corrupt our understanding of the past and in this way poison history.

Chapter 9
Conclusions

This volume has presented just a few examples of high-profile objects that either are or have been strongly suspected of being fakes, or are controversial for other reasons. It has attempted to draw out from each themes which are common to many such cases, but perhaps have particular resonance with particular cases. Creating copies of objects with the aim to deceive can certainly be seen to be nothing new. Cases are known from antiquity, and the oldest case presented here is the Turin Shroud, *if* this is indeed a fake. The Shroud is fascinating in that, although it has been known, and indeed questioned, for hundreds of years, of all the cases presented here it is the one with the least consensus as regards its attribution, with vehement supporters of both camps vocally putting their point of view. Certainly, at the time the Shroud *may* have been created, in the fourteenth century, there was almost an industry in the production of fake relics, driven by huge demand from churches and pilgrims and something of concern to the Church at the time. Other periods saw not so much deliberate fakery as a policy of copying early designs almost in homage to them. This is particularly true of the late Victorian period in the UK especially, where the "arts and crafts" movement and others celebrated the methods and styles of production of the medieval period. This produced objects that often cannot easily now be differentiated from the medieval originals. In the last fifty years the huge rise in the value of art, especially of paintings, has had an impact on the type and number of fakes and forgeries. The shear monetary gain of successfully selling a high-profile fake painting could now be seen as a huge incentive. However, this same period has seen a great increase in the application of science to the subject, so while it has certainly become more lucrative to pass off a fake as genuine, it has also become harder and more risky.

What can be faked? Well, it is clear that anything that can be made can be copied and therefore faked. However, there are some materials that are easier than others and there are some materials that are more difficult to detect as fakes than others. Perhaps the best material for the forger is stone. There are two cases concerning stone in this volume, and although both are probably now resolved as fakes, the work taken to do that, especially with the Getty Kouros, has been extensive. The main problem with stone for those attempting to determine whether the object was made yesterday or thousands of years ago is that only the external surface of the stone is changed in the manufacturing process. The main body (unlike for glass, ceramics, etc) is not changed. Thus, there is no dating technique that can help to date stone – you would be dating when the stone formed and not when the object was made. As can be seen in the case of the Kouros, a lot of effort has to be put into studying the surface of the stone to determine if that surface has spent centuries exposed to soil or weather, or if it has been artificially aged. The problem here is that every stone weathers differently, and different environments have the potential to cause different effects too. This is a relatively little-studied area, which adds to the difficulties. So stone is a particular problem for detecting fakes. The development of radiocarbon dating should have made it much more difficult to fake organic materials, since radiocarbon can be employed on "any material that once lived". However, there are still issues. The technique is destructive and requires a sample, which can be problematic, and there are other difficulties, as typified by the case of the Vinland Map. Here, the forger (if it is a forgery) has taken the trouble to find a parchment of the right date to work from and to "improve" by adding to it the map and the script. This reflects a common practice in the faking of paintings, where a canvas of the right period will be used and a new image placed upon it. Here, radiocarbon will say that only the parchment/canvas is of the right period, not the whole object. In the end, there are very few material types or objects that cannot be faked. Some are obviously rarer and more difficult than others, but that, in a way, almost acts as an advantage too. If a particular object type is very rarely faked, then it is far less likely that it will be subjected to the degree of scrutiny that a frequently faked type would be.

Why are objects faked? There might seem to be an obvious answer to this – for financial gain. This is undoubtedly true in some cases, where forgers were driven by a desire to generate as much money as they could from their works. However, there are often other, subtler drivers in the activities of forgers. Perhaps one of the most common, but complex, concerns the relationship of the forger with the art world that they are trying to fool. Forgers are talented people; they have to be or they would be immediately detected. They are artists in their own right and have often attempted to be artists in their own name, but have not been successful. This failure, as they see it, of the art world to recognise their talent can play a part in their decision to "go over to the dark side" and create fakes that will fool the world that has rejected them. Even where there is no such clear motive, there are other closely related issues that often do come out. There can frequently just be the joy of fooling people into believing that the object you have produced is a famous and important artwork. That might especially be the case if the forger is not formally trained. This might be seen in the case of the Amarna Princess, where it is difficult to believe that the forger, living on an estate in Bolton, did not derive pleasure from fooling major museums, collectors and connoisseurs with his work. Others have tried to use their work to gain access to, and be accepted by, just this establishment. Instead of seeing themselves as outsiders, "putting one over" on the elite, they have wanted to be members of it. This is part of the complex motivation behind the Piltdown forgery. Here the culprit was producing large numbers of objects which he was fraudulently using to gain access to museums and academic circles. He was certainly successful in this although, since he died relatively suddenly and young, it is unclear whether the outcome might have been different if he had continued with these activities – his chance of being discovered and of a scandal would surely have been high. A further possibility discussed in the volume is again similar – that there might be some element of a joke against the establishment in the activity. This has been suggested in the Piltdown case, but does not seem likely. It seems that this is more likely to be used as an excuse when the other motives here are more apposite – "it was just a joke, I did not think anyone would take it seriously" might be, and has been, used. Finally, there is a more complex motivation that might be seen. This is where a forger is genuinely trying to change history, perhaps genuinely believes that history is being misinterpreted and is attempting to "help" an interpretation by providing evidence, even if that evidence is fraudulent and self-generated. Perhaps this can be observed in the manufacturing of certain religious objects (although probably not the Shroud, even if it is medieval) and perhaps again in Piltdown and Vinland?

As well as an active and talented forger, the other vital part of a successful forgery is a receptive audience. A very significant part of the talent that a forger might have is not just the production of an object that withstands scrutiny, but also the production of a back story, or legend, that supports this. It is also thinking about the "mark", the victim and what they will believe. One of the points that should come out of this volume is that there is a victim in these crimes, a person or organisation whose reputation is at least diminished by their acceptance of the fake, by the mistake that they made. The best forgeries are very deliberately targeted at particular gaps in the market and can almost be personal in targeting individual academics and experts who the forger knows will be asked to comment on the object. A common way of both providing something of the legend for an object and acting as a hook for the unwary expert is to attempt to reproduce an object that is known from history, but has somehow been lost through time. The idea of discovering a "sleeper", a lost masterpiece that has been misattributed or simply hidden somewhere, is hugely attractive in the art world, whether to a curator or a dealer. This volume discusses perhaps the most extreme example of a sleeper ever found, the *Salvator Mundi*, a lost work by Leonardo and/or his studio, depending on critical opinion. While there is no suggestion that the *Salvator* is a fake, this sort of lost work would make an ideal target with which to tempt a mark into validating and buying it. The best fakes identify almost a need in the target to identify the object as what it is. Piltdown is another example of this. With no English hominid fossils found and good examples from the European mainland, there was both an expectancy and a need to find "the first Englishman". The forger fulfilled that need and the forgery went undiscovered for decades. Greenhalgh, the Bolton Forger, also specialised in trawling through early reports of works in academic journals and copying lost pieces for him or his family members to rediscover. This could be combined with pretend ignorance on the part of the person presenting the object to the museum or auction house. The line "I don't know what this is, do you think it is interesting?" and letting the mark discover the object in an early obscure journal has multiple benefits – firstly, the investment of time and effort into the story and the surprise and thrill of making an identification of an important object makes it difficult to question it logically and impartially. Secondly, if it is discovered as a fake, the forger has the hope of a defence since they never said that the object was genuine in the first place.

Finally, let us consider those whose business it is to detect and prevent fakes and forgeries at the front line. Here we have the connoisseur and the scientist. The connoisseur, whose long familiarity with the object type and period make them perhaps a world expert in the area, takes the lead on whether an object is right or wrong. As discussed in this volume, their long familiarity can mean that even they sometimes cannot articulate why something is not right; they just somehow *know*. Decades ago, this would have been enough for an object to sell, regardless of price. However, now (especially with very high value objects), it is increasingly common for the opinion of the connoisseur to be backed up by that of a scientist. In the ideal circumstances, these opinions will be completely independent.

Ideally, the scientist will not know the opinion of the connoisseur before undertaking the work. However, this rarely happens in practice – the scientist will usually know something of the connoisseur's concerns or otherwise beforehand. However, the techniques used will be completely different, the scientist drawing evidence from a different range of skills and resources. This resource will improve with time as equipment becomes better. This includes refinements in the development of existing analytical techniques where smaller (or no) samples are needed or detection limits and accuracy improve so that smaller differences between fakes and genuine objects can be identified. Occasionally, a brand-new technique appears, which can do things that were not thought possible before – the development of radiocarbon dating in the 1950s and then its AMS, small sample, improvement in the 1980s are an excellent example of a game-changing analytical tool. However, scientists publish their results and the way they detect forgeries becomes known in the trade. This allows forgers to work out new ways of fooling these techniques. What develops is essentially an arms race, where each side is trying to identify, understand and defeat the latest developments of the other. Working in such a thought-provoking and challenging area, where new developments and new forgeries come along on a regular basis, is one of the reasons why being a scientist working in the art world is such a rewarding and exciting role to have.

A Guided Bibliography

Many resources were used in the research for this book, and it is not intended that what follows should be exhaustive. However, readers who are particularly interested in certain cases might wish to look for further information on them, and this short annex will give some suggestions. It will also attempt to give some idea of how "mainstream" the opinion of the work is, or whether it is generally considered to be on the more imaginative end of interpretation. Of course, readers will be aware that this is based solely on the opinion of the authors of this book.

Scientific analysis

If the reader is interested in the methodologies that scientists use to investigate artworks, then there are several books on offer to look through. Without doubt, the best by a long way is *Scientific Investigation of Copies, Fakes and Forgeries.*[1] This was written by a scientist who spent decades at the British Museum Research Laboratory and worked on hundreds of objects, including many which had questions about their attribution. It is a comprehensive book, splitting the objects up by materials and discussing in detail how techniques are deployed and the results that can be gained from them. This is a first-class scholarly work (the references alone stretch for nearly 70 pages), but it is also readable. The author has many short case studies clearly shown in grey boxes, which makes it very easy to dip into. He also has an engaging sense of humour, which comes across well, particularly in the case studies. In an age of increasing specialisation amongst academics, we wonder whether anyone in future will have the broad scope of expertise and experience needed to write such a volume again. It is highly recommended. A very similar book, published within a year of the first, is *Scientific Methods and Cultural Heritage*.[2] This is also scholarly, with about the same number of pages of references and the same grey boxes, but it feels slightly more generalist, slightly less tightly tied to the objects and looking slightly more at a larger picture. It is more of a textbook than a handbook, but they are remarkably similar. A much lighter book is *The Scientist and the Forger*.[3] This does have some information about technique, but is much more about the art world and about the forgers themselves. Once again, many short case histories are given, but there is no intention here to go into the depths of material and scientific analysis that typify the other two books, especially the first.

[1] Craddock, P., 2009, *Scientific Investigation of Copies, Fakes and Forgeries*, Butterworth-Heinemann, Oxford.
[2] Artioli, G., 2010, *Scientific Methods and Cultural Heritage: an Introduction to the Application of Materials Science to Archaeometry and Conservation Science,* Oxford University Press, Oxford.
[3] Ragai, J., 2017, *The Scientist and the Forger: Probing a Turbulent Art World,* World Scientific, New Jersey, 2nd Edition.

Piltdown Man

There are many good books on Piltdown. If we start with the most contemporary, "primary" texts, then the place to start is undoubtedly the volume that showed that Piltdown was a fraud, *The Piltdown Forgery*.[1] First published in 1955, it is available in many subsequent printings by different publishers and with different prefaces and forewords by the great and the good. It is a good read, and clearly lays out the background and the case. Other good contemporary volumes describing Piltdown include Keith's *The Antiquity of Man*[2] which shows a senior scientist totally taken in by the forgery. Finally, of the early books one has to recommend Smith Woodward's own book, *The First Englishman*.[3] Written before the forgery was uncovered and unknowingly dedicated to the forger, this slim, little book is rather a sad reflection on the whole affair. The fact that Smith Woodward spent his last days writing this, "the last word was written the day before he died", as his wife tells us in the Prefactory Note, is particularly poignant.

Of the secondary sources, written at a later date about the case, a key text is *Piltdown, a Scientific Forgery*.[4] Wonderfully written, it presents a balanced account of the research on the case, with lots of excellent quotations from primary sources. It is accessible to the general reader, but with some meat for those more academically inclined. For those who want all the primary sources, then the companion volume, *The Piltdown Papers*,[5] could be added. For those interested in the other activities of Dawson, the forger, then there are some excellent books by Miles Russell, our favourite of which is the magnificently entitled *Piltdown Man: the Secret Life of Charles Dawson & the World's Greatest Archaeological Hoax*.[6] This details Russell's research on the myriad of other dodgy artefacts that Dawson produced and distributed. Finally, for those who are after more imaginative interpretations of who the perpetrator might be, these are listed and the cases against them disembowelled in *Piltdown, a Scientific Forgery*. However, special mention might be made of accusations against Arthur Conan Doyle, which somehow managed to get published in the leading scientific journal, *Science*,[7] – it must have been a slow news day.

[1] Weiner, J.S., 1955, *The Piltdown Forgery*, Oxford University Press, Oxford.

[2] Keith, A., 1915, *The Antiquity of Man*, Williams and Norgate, London.

[3] Smith Woodward, A., 1948, *The First Englishman*, Watts and Co, London.

[4] Spencer, F., 1990, *Piltdown, a Scientific Forgery*, British Museum (Natural History) and Oxford University Press, London, Oxford and New York.

[5] Spencer, F., 1990, *The Piltdown Papers*, British Museum (Natural History) and Oxford University Press, London, Oxford and New York.

6   Russell, M., 2003, *Piltdown Man: the Secret Life of Charles Dawson &*
     the World's Greatest Archaeological Hoax, Tempus, Stroud.

7   Winslow, J. and Myer, A., 1983, The perpetrator of Piltdown, *Science*,
     83.4, 32-43.

Getty Kouros

The work done on the Kouros was carried out almost entirely at The Getty and published mostly by it or at its instigation. A key text is *The Getty Kouros Colloquium*, the account of the meeting of scholars held in Athens in 1992. It is available for free online from the Getty website[1] and is an excellent starting point to learn more about the various opinions on the Kouros. Another interesting area to look at is the various newspaper articles on the subject that are available free online, especially in the *LA Times*.

On the more general subject of the looting of antiquities, there are now a myriad of books that give an opinion in this area. We would recommend two as important in the exposure of the complicity of major museums and auction houses in not carrying out full due diligence on suspect pieces and their provenance. The first, *Sotheby's: Inside Story*,[1] was published in 1997 and details specific cases where auction houses have been suspected of selling looted and smuggled objects. It is an excellent piece of investigative journalism and remains readable. However, if one were to read only one book concerning the problems of looted material and the implications for and involvement of US museums, then it should be *Chasing Aphrodite*.[3] While covering other scandals in other museums, this is the story of the curators, lawyers and directors of The Getty Museum, and their attempts to make The Getty one of the best museums in the world, sometimes by methods that were highly questionable.

1   http://www.getty.edu/publications/virtuallibrary/0892362634.html

2   Watson, P., 1997, *Sotheby's: Inside Story*, Bloomsbury, London.

3   Felch, J. and Frammelino, R., 2011, *Chasing Aphrodite, the hunt for*
     looted antiquities at the World's richest museum, HMH, New York.

Turin Shroud

The degree of controversy over the Shroud is matched only by the sheer number of publications that its study has produced. The literature on all the other cases discussed in this volume *put together* does not come close to matching the amount written about the Shroud. This is therefore an even more partial list than those for the other cases. Perhaps the best place to start is at the heart of the controversy, the radiocarbon date, published in *Nature*[1] in a relatively short paper that is easy to read and gives the key details. The background to the Shroud and its history is well documented in many accounts, but perhaps our favourite are the books written by Ian Wilson,[2] who quite fairly records what is known (or not), although his attempts to link the Shroud with other religious objects and thus stretch its history backwards are less mainstream.

For early scientific work on the Shroud, there are some details in a *National Geographic* article,[3] but a lot of the material is not published. A remarkable resource for all things that relate to the Shroud is the "Shroud of Turin Website",[4] where a lot of details of the Shroud's history, and especially its investigation, are to be found. It is a popular site, with nearly nine million views in March 2021. However (and it is a big however), it needs to be read carefully. Some of the material is balanced and mainstream in its views, whilst other parts are absolutely not. Read with the right attitude of scepticism (for both sides of the argument) it can be regarded as a powerful resource for those interested in the subject. As the editor points out, the opinions expressed on the website are not necessarily those of the editor. The website has a very long list of books on the Shroud, including many iterations of the work of Ian Wilson, the most recent of which was published in 2010.[2] It is interesting to note that he has also written extensively on reincarnation and after-death experience. From the more scientific point of view, the best text on the background to the radiocarbon date and its immediate aftermath is *Relic, Icon or Hoax*.[5] Written by Harry Gove, who was central to the setting up of the dating protocol, but then not involved in the actual dating itself, it gives the background to the disputes amongst the scientists about how the Shroud should be dated and the dangers of using only three laboratories rather than the larger number originally wanted. It looks prescient in its predictions of potential disputes and attacks on the date, although solid in asserting that the date is right. For a more imaginative reflection on the Shroud as a medieval copy, try *Turin Shroud: In Whose Image? The Shocking Truth Unveiled*.[6] Here the authors attempt to show that the Shroud is in fact a photograph taken by Leonardo da Vinci. Leonardo was not born until 1452, so well outside the most likely range for the radiocarbon date. This is a rare example of a work that neither side in the argument, genuine or copy, is going to be happy with.

[1]   Damon, *et al.*, 1989, Radiocarbon Dating the Shroud of Turin, *Nature*, 337, 302.

[2]   Wilson, I., 2010, *The Shroud: The 2000-Year-Old Mystery Solved*, Bantam, London.

[3]   Weaver, K.F., 1980, The Mystery of the Shroud, *National Geographic*, June, 730-52.

[4]   https://www.shroud.com

[5]   Gove, H.E., 1996, *Relic, Icon or Hoax? Radiocarbon Dating the Turin Shroud*, Institute of Physics, Bristol and Philadelphia.

[6]   Picknett, L. and Prince, C., 1994, *Turin Shroud: In Whose Image? The Shocking Truth Unveiled*, Bloomsbury, London.

Vinland Map

The original text of the Vinland Map and the Tartar Relation has been reprinted, supported by introductions and essays on the Map's provenance and authenticity.[1]

Most of the scientific analyses performed on the Map and the manuscript, raising doubts about or downright denying the authenticity of the Vinland Map, have been published in a myriad of specialised scientific journals. These analytical papers focus more on the scientific methodology used, rather than the object itself. Perhaps the book *Maps, Myths and Men* by Kirsten Seaver gives the best accessible account of the earlier investigations[2] (and summarises why the Vinland Map would be a forgery). The most recent summary of several decades of work on the Map can be found in the integral recording of the Mystic Seaport Museum symposium held in 2018, which can be watched online.[3] The Beinecke Library at Yale University, after its most recent analysis, certainly considers the map to be a twentieth-century forgery.

[1] Skelton, R.A., et al., 1995, *The Vinland Map and the Tartar Relation* (2nd ed.), Yale University Press, New Haven CT.

[2] Seaver, K.A., 2004, *Maps, Myths and Men*, Stanford University Press, Stanford CA.

[3] https://www.youtube.com/watch?app=desktop&v=z1YXS8dbY-2Id%2F

Amarna Princess

Compared to other written material on other objects here, the Amarna princess, being relatively recent, obviously has a lot less written about it. What is, though, is interesting. The main reference to the reason the statue was identified as a fake is written by the curator involved, unfortunately in a rather obscure publication,[1] but gives an excellent background to the case. It also crops up in passing in other works, and one particularly to note is *Egyptian Fakes*.[2] This is an interesting and approachable account of the history of faking Egyptian antiquities including a number of famous cases. As mentioned in the chapter itself, the Amarna princess is a rare example where the forger himself has written about his activities. *A Forger's Tale*[3] received some good reviews ("told with wit and charm", "a likable voice" and "has an eye for detail"). Remarkably, it was featured in the *Observer's* best art books list of 2018, although perhaps as a comedy afterthought. We found it turgid and too long. It also does not give the level of detail that we wanted on how objects were researched, raw materials acquired and, generally, objects made. For us it was a disappointing book. The question of how true some of it is pops into one's mind throughout. The claiming of *La Bella Principessa* is particularly eye-catching and the scholarly attribution of this to Leonardo is also worth reading.[4] Finally, the television programmes featuring Greenhalgh are also worth a view.[5] Although now slightly difficult to find, they are available on YouTube and elsewhere.

[1] Hardwick, T., 2010, A Group of Art Works in the Amarna Style, in D'Auria, S.H. (ed.), *Offerings to the Discerning Eye. An Egyptological Medley in Honor of Jack A. Josephson*, Brill, Leiden and Boston, 133-51.

[2] Fiechter, J.J., 2009, *Egyptian Fakes: Masterpieces that Duped the Art World and the Experts who Uncovered them*, Flammarion, Paris.

[3] Greenhalgh, S., 2015, *A Forger's Tale: Confessions of the Bolton Forger*, Bell and Bain, Glasgow.

[4] Kemp, M. and Cotte, P., 2010, *Leonardo da Vinci, La Bella Principessa: the Profile Portrait of a Milanese Woman*, Hodder and Stoughton, London.

[5] "Handmade in Bolton", made for BBC4 https://www.bbc.co.uk/programmes/m00095hs.

Leonardo

There are many biographies and studies of Leonardo, but one of the most enduring is *Leonardo da Vinci* by Kenneth Clarke.[1] Clarke is perhaps the connoisseur's connoisseur, and his writing is eloquent and comprehensive. His opinion of the *oeuvre* he discusses is still relevant today, eighty years after publication. On the subject of the Leonardo that is the centre of this chapter there are two texts. The first to appear was *The Last Leonardo*,[2] which rather scooped the later official production. It is an interesting and engaging book, telling the story of the painting from the point of view of an outsider – an investigative journalist. It is the easier of the books to read on the subject. The second volume is *Leonardo's Salvator Mundi & the collecting of Leonardo in the Stuart courts*,[3] and can be regarded as the official history of what happened by those who were directly involved. Its publication was delayed, it appearing only six months or so after *The Last Leonardo*. It is a more scholarly work and, as the subtitle suggests, goes into the detail of the early history of the collecting of this painting and others.

For those more interested in connoisseurs, Martin Kemp's auto-biography[4] is worth a read. It tells of his work on Leonardo, but just as much of the relationships between connoisseurs, scholars, the public and, as the cover puts it, "pseudo-historians, fantasists [and] swelling legions of Leonardo loonies". He is, as always, not afraid to give his opinion. Finally, we would like to mention one work by Hugh Trevor-Roper. It is a huge shame that his career was blighted by some unwise decisions, and so we would like to recommend what we regard as one of his most important works. A brilliant scholar, employed in intelligence during and after the Second World War, his *The Last Days of Hitler*[5] comprehensively proved that Hitler was dead for all those for whom such an outcome was popular. It is a superb piece of work and is an accessible read, even today.

[1]   Clarke, K., 2005, *Leonardo da Vinci*, Foilio, London.

[2]   Lewis, B., 2019, *The Last Leonardo: the secret lives of the World's most expensive painting*, Collins, London.

[3]   Dalivalle, M., Kemp, M. and Simon, R.B., *Leonardo's Salvator Mundi & the collecting of Leonardo in the Stuart courts*, Oxford University Press, UK

[4]   Kemp, M., 2018, *Living with Leonardo: fifty years of sanity and insanity in the art world and beyond*, Thames and Hudson, UK.

[5]   Trevor-Roper, H-R. and Tedder, A.W., 1947, *The last days of Hitler*, Macmillan, New York.

Knossos

Many scientific papers and other books have been written on the restoration of Knossos, but an excellent resource on the excavations and reconstruction is the exhibit on Knossos in the Ashmolean

Museum of Oxford University. Here, the story and motivation of the main people involved are well explained and clearly visualised, and perhaps better framed than at the site itself. The vintage original publications by Arthur Evans can be both enlightening and entertaining, for instance the successive volumes from the 1920s and 1930s entitled *The Palace of Minos: a comparative account of the successive stages of the early Cretan civilization as illustrated by the discoveries at Knossos*. These were published by Macmillan and Co of London, but are available via open access on the internet, and give a nostalgic yet insightful glimpse of what was common as scientific publication at the beginning of the twentieth century. The description of the site of Knossos and other Minoan palatial centres on the UNESCO cultural World Heritage Tentative List makes for an interesting read on the retained value of the site.[1] The ICOMOS (International Council on Monuments and Sites) website[2] is well stocked with explanation and publications around the conservation of monuments and heritage, and links to themes such as sustainable development and climate change. It also has information on national committees, and gives regional information. Detailed and accessible information on the undergraduate student level on the topics of conservation and anastylosis can be found in *Architectural Conservation*[3] by Aylin Orbasli and *Conservation of Ruins*[4] by John Ashurst.

[1] http://whc.unesco.org/en/tentativelists/5860/
[2] https://www.icomos.org/
[3] Orbasli, A., 2007, Architectural Conservation: Principles and Practice, Wiley-Blackwell, London.
[4] Ashurst, J., 2009, Conservation of Ruins, Routledge, London.

Glossary

Key Museums

The Art Institute of Chicago: https://www.artic.edu/
Ashmolean Museum: https://www.ashmolean.org/
Barkham Manor: http://www.berkshirehistory.com/castles/barkham_manor.html
Beinecke Rare Book and Manuscript Library: https://beinecke.library.yale.edu/
Bolton Museum: https://www.boltonlams.co.uk/museum
Boston Museum of Fine Art: https://www.mfa.org/
British Museum: https://www.britishmuseum.org/
British Museum (Natural History): also the Natural History Museum https://www.nhm.ac.uk/
Louvre Museum: https://www.louvre.fr/en
Metropolitan Museum of Art: https://www.metmuseum.org/
Mystic Seaport Museum: https://www.mysticseaport.org/
National Etruscan Museum: https://www.museoetru.it/
National Gallery London: https://www.nationalgallery.org.uk/
Victoria and Albert Museum: https://www.vam.ac.uk/

Key individuals

Cardinal Anastasio Ballestrero (1913-1998): Anastasio del Santissimo Rosario, Italian Roman Catholic cardinal, Archbishop of Turin from 1977 to 1989, who allowed testing of the Turin Shroud.

Gianfranco Becchina (1939-): Italian antiquities dealer, now olive oil producer, involved in controversy around illegal dealing in artifacts.

Robin Clark (1935-2018): New Zealand (Britain-based) chemist and professor, who pioneered Raman spectroscopy. He is widely known for his work in art authentication.

Charles Darwin (1809-1882): British naturalist, best known for his book *On the Origin of Species* and his contributions to the theory of evolution.

Charles Dawson (1864-1916): British solicitor and amateur palaeontologist, best known for a number of archaeological and palaeontological discoveries which turned out to be forgeries.

Christian Charles Tyler Doll (1880-1955): British architect, replacing Theodore Fyfe for the restorations of Knossos.

Sir Arthur Evans (1851-1941): British archaeologist and Keeper of the Ashmolean Museum, pioneering the study of Aegean civilisations and languages in the Bronze age. Widely known for his excavations and reconstitutions at the Cretan site of Knossos.

Barbara and Lawrence Fleischman (1924-, 1925-1997): American art collectors and philanthropists.

Mechthild Flury-Lemberg (1929-): Swiss conservator and restorer, expert in ancient textile and cloth.

Jiri Frel (1923-2006): Czech-American curator of the J. Paul Getty Museum, credited with the expansion of its antiquities collection, but involved in controversy around the acquisitions' purchase and origin.

David Theodore Fyfe (1875-1945): British architect, working on the initial restorations of Knossos with Sir Arthur Evans between 1900 and 1904.

John Paul Getty (1892-1976): American-British oil industrialist and collector of art. Founded the J. Paul Getty Trust and related museum complex.

Harry Gove (1922-2009): Canadian nuclear physicist and professor, heavily involved in the development of radiometric dating techniques.

Shaun Greenhalgh (1961-): British artist and prolific former art forger.

Edward Thomas (Teddy) Hall, CBE (1924-2001): British chemist and scientist, professor and founder of the Research Laboratory for Archaeology and the History of Art at Oxford University.

Robert Hecht (1919-2012): American antiquities and art dealer based in Europe, involved in controversy around looted artifacts.

Piet de Jong (1887-1967): Dutch artist, replacing Christian Doll as architect at Knossos, active from 1922 to 1952, designing and directing much of the restoration works.

Martin Kemp (1942-): British art historian and emeritus professor, world authority on Leonardo da Vinci.

Ernst Langlotz (1895-1978): German archaeologist, specialising in Greek sculpture of the 6th to 5th centuries BCE.

Thomas Marston (1905-1984): American curator of medieval and Renaissance literature at Yale University library.

Walter McCrone (1916-2002): American chemist, expert in microscopy, widely known for his work in forensic science and on forged art and antiquities.

Paul Mellon (1907-1999): American investor and philanthropist, major benefactor in the art and academic world.

Dianne Dwyer Modestini: American professor and painting conservator, specialising in Old Masters.

Alexander Parish: New York-based art dealer, joint former owner of the *Salvator Mundi*.

Jerry Podany: American retired head of antiquities conservation of the J. Paul Getty Museum. Active as conservation consultant still.

Jussi Pylkkanen (1963-): Finnish art dealer and global president of the Christie's auction house.

Erwin Schroedinger (1887-1961): Austrian Nobel Prize-winning physicist and professor, best known for his work on quantum theory and the Schroedinger's Cat thought experiment.

Robert Simon: New York-based art dealer, Robert Simon Fine Art Inc., joint former owner of the *Salvator Mundi*.

Sir Arthur Smith Woodward (1864-1944): British palaeontologist, expert in fossil fish. Keeper of the Geology department of the British Museum Natural History.

Father Marie-Joseph Pierre Teilhard de Chardin (1881-1955): French Jesuit priest, palaeontologist and archaeologist, known as the author of philosophical and theological books.

Michael Tite (1938-): British physicist and archaeological scientist, active at the British Museum and later professor at the Research Laboratory for Archaeology and the History of Art of Oxford University.

Hugh Trevor-Roper, Baron Dacre of Glanton (1914-2003): British historian and professor, widely known for his book *The last days of Hitler*, but involved in controversy around the forged *Hitler Diaries*.

Marion True (1948-): American former curator of antiquities for the J. Paul Getty Museum, entangled in controversy around the purchase and provenance of artifacts.

Leonardo da Vinci (1452-1519): Italian Renaissance inventor, architect-engineer, scientist, painter, artist… who pioneered observations and research on a great variety of subjects.

Laurence Claiborne Witten II (1926-1995): American book dealer and art collector, involved in the controversy around the purchase and origin of the Vinland Map at Yale University.

Frederico Zeri (1921-1998): Italian art historian, specialising in Renaissance painting and known for denouncing forgeries.

Key terms

Absolute Age: the actual number of years that have elapsed from an event until now.

Acheulian: type of archaeological industry of stone tools during the Pleistocene.

Alabaster: sedimentary rock type, composed of calcite or gypsum. The term is used in different ways by archaeologists and geologists.

Amarna: sometimes Tell el-Amarna; capital of ancient Egypt, newly built around 1346 BCE by Akhenaten, King of Egypt.

Analytical protocol: full procedure of analysis, from obtaining the material for analysis and choice of analytical technique to the full preparation procedure and quality check of the data obtained.

Anastylosis: reconstruction technique in which original parts are used to the greatest degree possible.

Anatase: mineral form (one out of three occurring in nature) of titanium dioxide (TiO_2).

The Archaeological Institute of America: learned society for the advancement of archaeological sites and cultural heritage, promoting the ethical practice of archaeology; https://www.archaeological.org/

Atom: smallest unit of an element in the periodic table of elements that retains the element's physical and chemical properties.

Atomic mass: the sum of an element's protons and neutrons.

Atomic number: the number of protons in the nucleus of an atom, defining the place and name of the element in the periodic table of elements.

Australopithecus africanus: extinct species of hominids, which lived during the middle Pliocene to early Pleistocene.

Bronze: metal alloy of copper and tin.

Calcite: mineral composed of calcium carbonate ($CaCO_3$).

Canine tooth: fang-like sharp, pointed teeth between incisors and molars, used to tear food.

Carbon dating: method of absolute dating, measuring the decay of the carbon isotope ^{14}C. Conventional carbon dating measures the radiation emitted in this decay process, while AMS-based radiocarbon dating performs a detailed isotopic analysis using Accelerated Mass Spectrometry.

Confidence interval: range of values with an associated probability level (e.g. 95% confidence level) giving the likelihood with which the estimated interval will contain the true value of a parameter.

Conservation science: interdisciplinary field concerned with the care and protection of cultural works.

Contamination: presence of an impurity or undesirable element that may spoil the evaluation of an object or sample.

Cosmic rays: high energy particles and radiation moving through space and reaching Earth from outside the planet.

Cranium: skull, especially the part of the hominid facial skeleton enclosing the brain.

Dolomite: mineral composed of calcium magnesium carbonate ($CaMg[CO_3]_2$).

Electron: a negatively charged particle, with a charge -1, that moves around the nucleus of an atom.

Electron microscopy: imaging technique making use of electrons to scan and image the surface of objects.

Eoanthropus dawsoni: also Piltdown Man.

Eoliths: chipped stone, usually flint, believed to be the earliest stone tools made, but now regarded as naturally occurring.

Fluorine test: method of dating based on the absorption of fluorine in buried objects, mostly used to relatively compare objects.

FTIR: analytical technique making use of infrared radiation to evaluate the nature of chemical bonds to identify substances present.

Geochronology: discipline within the geosciences, devoted to the dating of rocks and geological processes.

the Geological Society: UK national society for geoscience; https://www.geolsoc.org.uk/

Gypsum: mineral composed of hydrated calcium sulphate ($CaSO_4.2H_2O$).

Hominid: member of the biological family Hominidae, the taxonomical family of primates.

Homo Heidelbergensis: extinct species of hominids, an archaic human, which lived during the middle Pleistocene.

Infrared: form of electromagnetic radiation with an energy just lower and wavelength higher than visible light.

Ion: atom that is electrically charged through the loss or gain of electrons.

Iron gall ink: ink made of iron slats and tannic acids of vegetable origin (e.g. sumac leaves or gallnuts).

Isotope (of an element): species of atoms with the same atomic number but with different atomic masses.

Isotopic analysis: measurement of the ratio of abundance of two isotopes.

Ivy League: Eight Northeastern US universities (Brown, Columbia, Cornell, Dartmouth, Harvard, Pennsylvania, Princeton and Yale), considered excellent academic institutions for learning and research.

Keeper: curator in a cultural heritage institution, involved in the conservation and interpretation of the materials.

Kouros: statue of a single naked youth, 7th to 5th centuries CE, Greece.

Limestone: biochemical sedimentary rock type, composed mainly of fossils and the mineral calcite, but may also include dolomite (and is then often called a dolostone).

Lithification: the process that converts loose sediment to solid rock by compaction and cementation by chemical processes.

Magma: molten rock, when above ground called lava.

Magmatic rock: rock type formed from the cooling and solidification of magma.

Mandible: lower jawbone in the hominid facial skeleton.

Mandylion: relic showing the face of Christ.

Marble: metamorphic rock type, metamorphic equivalent of limestone or dolostone.

Metamorphic rock: rock type formed from the transformation of pre-existing rocks under the influence of high (geological) pressure and/or temperature.

Mass spectrometry: analytical technique separating, measuring and quantifying species (isotopes, atoms or molecules) of different mass.

Mastodon: elephant-like animal of the Mammut genus, extinct at the end of the Pleistocene.

Microprobe: analytical technique measuring the chemical composition of materials by measuring the characteristic X-rays emitted by this material after excitation with charged particles such as electrons or ions.

Mineral: a naturally occurring, solid, crystalline substance with a specific chemical composition between certain boundaries.

Minoans: Bronze Age Aegean civilisation, flourishing between the 3rd and 1st millennia CE.

Mohs scale of hardness: empirical ascending scale of mineral hardness, based on the ability of a mineral to scratch another.

Neo-Gothic: 18th to 19th century architectural movement, reviving medieval Gothic architecture.

Neo-classical: 18th century architectural movement, reviving Greco-Roman-style architecture.

Neutron: an electrically neutral elementary particle in the nucleus of an atom, having an atomic mass of 1.

Nineveh: ancient Assyrian city in Mesopotamia, near Mosul in modern-day Iraq.

Nucleus: the centre of an atom, comprising protons and neutrons, containing virtually all the mass of the atom.

Palaeoanthropology: branch of archaeology, palaeontology and anthropology investigating the development of anatomically modern humans.

Parietal lobe: part of the cerebral cortex of the mammal brain, important in processing sensory information. The left parietal is essential in developing language skills.

Patina: layer on the outside of rocks caused by chemical and physical alteration or weathering, in contact with the atmosphere or burial environment.

Pernicious anaemia: disease impairing the uptake of vitamin B12 in the body, eventually causing organ damage.

Piltdown Painting: painting by John Cooke, 1915, showing the people involved in the discovery of *Eoanthropus dawsoni.*

PIXE: Particle Induced X-ray Emission, analysis technique similar to microprobe, using an ion beam to induce X-ray emission in a material typical of its chemical composition.

Pleistocene: geological epoch, from around 2.5 million years to 11.800 years ago.

Pliocene: geological epoch, from around 5.3 million years to around 2.5 million years ago.

Pollen: microscopic grains discharged from plants, which play a role in their reproductive process.

Proton: elementary particle in the nucleus of an atom, having an atomic mass of 1 and a positive electrical charge of +1.

Provenance: documentation tracing an object back to its source and owners, or the origin of the raw materials used to make an object.

Quarry: extraction site of geological materials such as stone.

Quartzite: hard metamorphic rock, originating from the recrystallisation of quartz-rich sandstone.

Radioactive decay: the process by which an unstable isotope loses energy by radiation, evolving into a more stable isotope.

Raman: analytical technique making use of laser radiation to evaluate the nature of chemical bonds to identify substances present.

Restoration: reconstitution to an cleaned or more original state of a work of art or archaeological object.

Rock: an aggregate of one or more types of minerals.

Sample: limited amount of a substance or object, fit for analysis and meant to represent the whole.

Sandstone: clastic rock composed of grains of quartz, feldspar and other minerals or rock fragments with a grain size of between 64 μm and 2 mm, naturally cemented together. The lithified equivalent of sand.

Sedimentary rock: rock type formed from the deposition and possibly lithification of layers of sediment (such as sand, other rock fragments, fossils).

Society of Antiquaries: learned society for the study and knowledge of antiquities and their history; https://www.sal.org.uk/

Soil: a weathering product of bedrock, composed of rock fragments, newly formed (clay) minerals and organic matter.

Sudarium: sweat cloth to wipe the face with, here mentioned in relation to the Passion of Jesus Christ.

Templars: also "Order of Solomon's Temple" or "Knights Templar", medieval military-religious order defending Jerusalem and pilgrim routes into that city.

Ultraviolet: form of electromagnetic radiation with an energy just higher and wavelength shorter than visible light.

Vandyke brown: also Cologne earth, brown pigment originally made from soil, later from petroleum products.

Villa dei Papiri: ancient Roman luxurious house, excavated in Herculanuem (Italy).

the Weald: area in south-east England.

Weathering: a series of chemical and physical alteration processes, breaking up rock into smaller fragments or dissolving its mineral components.

CPSIA information can be obtained
at www.ICGtesting.com
Printed in the USA
LVHW080018150722
723584LV00014B/903